DADDY SIR!
By
Christine McAteer

Published by

Willow Entertainment

All Rights Reserved

No part of this book may be reproduced in any form by photocopying or any electronic or mechanical means, including information storage or retrieval systems, without permission in writing from the publisher of this book.

2nd Edition published 2019

Christine McAteer

ISBN 9781079298017

Contact author at willentllc@gmail.com

To Terry

All my love,

All my life

Chris

Forward

Child sexual abuse is a global problem. In the US, it is estimated that as many as one out of five girls are sexually abused. In Christine McAteer's searing memoir, we see from the inside how this trauma is experienced. Deeply in touch with her childhood memories, McAteer shows what she felt as a little girl. This book reveals how abuse takes place in specific places and in the context of relationships. Ninety percent of victims know their abusers; thirty percent are like Christine, abused by members of their own family.

Her story reveals a haunting sense of place where the child faces both the reality of her presence there and the unreality of her body being used and betrayed. She describes her memory of herself as "a ghost child, a thin little girl watchful, wary, and afraid." (1-2). McAteer the writer uses the details of her experience symbolically. The physical objects reflect her psyche's ruin: the abandoned piano in her grandparents' yard suggests how she wanted to sing but was silenced. McAteer leads us fully into the terror and loss of her early life. With her, we feel the dreaded sound of her father's tires crunching on the gravel, which means he is home, and there will be beatings and an assault. She describes every sight and scent and touch. Vividly she recalls Daddy's curses and commands. However hard she worked, he punished her for falling short. She tells her story from the innocent perspective of the young girl she was.

Her story is unrelenting but important to anyone who has been sexually abused as a child and to those who know and love them. Her abuse started when she was just two and continued through high school. She lived in the country in Smithfield, Texas. Like her, those living in rural areas have twice the rate of abuse as those living elsewhere. And many other factors conflate the abuse: poverty, gender, birth order, the mother's illnesses and alcoholism, family history. Her father, older brother, uncle, and grandfather all molested her. One of seven children, when she moved out her father began abusing her younger sister.

Her resilience and her innocence in some ways sheltered her though they could not protect her. Her book is filled with her love of sunshine, animals, her joy at being in school and smelling the chalk and newly washed blackboard, the scent of her pink pencil eraser, and her memories of singing with her parents and the special delights of Christmas with a huge, real Christmas tree. She recounts how she loved to go with her brother to pick blackberries:

> Bees hummed close by, singing in the early summer stillness. Mockingbirds called to one another in the trees and a small green lizard slithered over my foot It was a deliciously cool morning, and the sun shone gently warm. My heart began to feel content. I ate some of the sweet berries. They slid sweetly down my throat and stained my mouth with purple juice. Here among the berries, Daddy seemed far, far away. (23)

She writes with a poet's sensuous detail and sensitivity and then brings us back to reality with a shock. Her days of contentment were the backdrop to her nights of pain and shame.

It is not only the specific descriptions of her abuse that we learn from but her inner feelings—of pleasure, of pain, and guilt. In the later chapters of this book, she shows how these emotions do not end when the abuse does. They affect every aspect of her life. Her father and others violated the very nature of childhood by robbing her of trust, affection, and safety. She was never abused by someone she did not love.

Let that sink in.

She was the responsible and good girl who looked after her siblings, the house, and her parents. But she also was the one who was called a "goddamn liar" and "dirty."

And there was no one to tell. She writes of the bond of secrecy. Don't tell your teachers. Don't tell your mother. Don't tell your brothers. Or grandmother. Or priest. Or friends. In fact, sixty percent of abused children never confide in anyone.

Women who have been abused develop low self-esteem, a feeling of worthlessness, a distorted view of sex, and are three times more likely to abuse drugs or alcohol. In the

US, forty percent of women who were abused as children are alcoholics vs. fourteen percent of women not abused as girls. Christine has had to overcome this too.

McAteer shows how she left home early to escape the attacks, and she married young. Sex with her husband was painful. Her husband encouraged her to use drugs. He was deeply dependent on her. Later they both joined the Army, where their marriage ended while her vulnerability and willingness to please exposed her to other men's exploitation of her. From her minister to her sergeant, Chris recounts how she could not say no. Her body had never been entirely hers, so she could not fully claim it or enforce her boundaries even as an adult woman.

In time, the repressed memories emerged in nightmares and in multiple personalities. She describes how she developed thirty-two alters, many of them "littles" or children. And she tried to take care of all of them. Anyone dealing with dissociative identity disorder (DID) also will learn from Chris' account.

But this is not a story of defeat. The courage of this writer, who revisits these scenes of terror and loss, is immense. She does it for a purpose—to help others who have endured it and to educate those who want to understand. Through therapy, journaling, confiding in others, hospitalization, and getting psychological help from qualified therapists, Chris shows how to live her life. She writes how essential is the "pulling apart the pain and memories and looking them in the eye." (160).

Reading this book is not easy, but it is necessary. More children are raped than adults. Sexual assaults and abuse of children are all too common. But Chris McAteer shows that healing is possible. She will always struggle in some ways to overcome what she endured long ago. But by encountering the pain she shares in this memoir, she regains herself. She writes, "Ever so gently I am removing the dirt and rubble, shifting through the mess to find treasures that might otherwise be lost. I slowly brought the damaged pieces to life and repaired them with infinite care." (189). That is the purpose of this book—that through the pain will come new life.

Dr. Sherida Yoder,

**Professor of English,
Felician University**

Introduction

Daddy Sir! is a memoir of survival and hope. It is the story of how I survived severe sexual, physical, and emotional abuse. It is a story of dissociative identity disorder (DID) and a story of post-traumatic stress disorder (PTSD).

Eighteen years ago, I was in enough pain to start therapy. I was just coming out of a failed marriage and entering a new one. I was abusing alcohol and the symptoms of DID and PTSD had intensified to the extent that I could not hold a job. I was self-destructing.

Heather, my first therapist helped me to identify the thirty-two alter personalities that were fragmenting my life. She pulled me away from the abyss of pain and began to inject some healing into my tormented days. Heather died at a crucial point in my therapy and I went from therapist to therapist during the next 10 years. My hunt finally brought me to Tana who helped me become much healthier and I began to heal from the splits of the alter personalities.

Buddhism and meditation have entered my life. Meditation is how I really began to process my feelings. These were feelings of self-hatred, depression, and fear. Through therapy and meditation, I felt them fully and released pain. I have entered a new world of healing, happiness and wellbeing.

The reason why I wrote my life story is because I needed to process the story and I needed to feel like my life meant something. Reading this book is not an easy journey. Frankly there are chapters that are very difficult to read but they are truthful chapters. I did not sugar coat any of the abuse. That would have helped no one.

I hope this book accomplishes two things. One, if you are an abuse survivor, I hope it helps you to see that you do not suffer alone and that healing, wholeness, and a happy life are possible. My second hope is that if you are reading this and you are close to a survivor it helps you to understand the extreme emotional damage that occurs with sexual abuse.

      Finally, my story is not uncommon. Sexual abuse could be happening in the home of your best friend, or your next-door neighbor, or the house across the street. Many victims are terrorized by their perpetrators and have no voice. I suffered incest for seventeen years and never cried out for help. I was afraid. The child in your classroom may be afraid as well. I have given my experience a voice and I hope it touches you.

CHAPTER ONE
JOURNEY HOME

Time had ravaged and changed Grandmother's front yard. I stood alone under the tree where, as a little girl, I had spent so many hours playing tea party with my dolls. Weeds now choked that once familiar yard, but some areas of the property were still intact. There was the porch where I had played as a child, now dilapidated and falling into ruin. The windmill still rose tall above the house; it's once whirling wings now silent. The old well had long since been boarded over for safety. Strings exposed, an abandoned, rotting piano sat under the big tree where I stood and wondered if it was the one that had sat in our living room for so many years. The ancient elm tree in front of the empty house groaned in lonely protest as the wind violated her old branches.

I stood in silence my mind crowded with unbidden memories. Although someone had screened the front porch, the barn still stood out far in the back, falling down now and badly in need of paint. The wooden garage that had housed the old red Chevy was still there. I walked up the gravel drive and looked through the door. Coiled ropes and dirty wooden boxes covered the dirt floor. I continued my journey to the house, aware of my husband standing behind me.

I stepped carefully onto the porch. Wood splintered and an old rusty dog ran out from under the house. It was the sight of the dog that almost undid me.

"Oh, Charles," I cried, "a dog! Granddaddy always kept a dog under the house!"

"Be careful, Chris," Charles warned. "This porch is really rotten. Besides, you don't know who lives here now."

"But it looks abandoned!" I cried, "Everything is falling down." Then, noticing the padlock on the door I tried to look through the window but could see nothing.

I left the porch and walked around the side of the house. Walking beside me was a ghost child, a thin little girl watchful, wary, and afraid. I softly took her hand and did my best to reassure her. I knew who she was, and I would not allow her to be hurt. She and I had suffered enough. I came to what appeared to be a bedroom window and saw a torn and dirty mattress lying on the floor. Evidently the house was now occupied by transients.

"Hell is for children," I softly sang the words to the song under my breath as we left grandmother's yard and began to walk along the highway. I tightened the grip of my hand upon that of the trembling ghost child as we proceeded down this highway of my childhood memories. I was trembling inside. More confrontation of my past lay ahead.

We stood at the edge of the property that was my childhood home. A part of my mind recorded that I was really in Smithfield, Texas, and that after a space of 24 years, I had finally come home. The trees whispered and sighed. I noticed that the grapevines still grew along the edge of the property. Instead of the long straight drive that ended at the road of my memory, I saw a circular driveway well maintained. Most of the trees that had surrounded the house were gone. I smiled as I remembered the "treasure" we children had buried beneath those trees.

The small white house was gone as well. In its place a sprawling ranch house loomed tall and important. By looking carefully, I could barely see the framework of the original structure hidden in its sprawling outlines. In my mind's eye I could see several small and dirty children playing around that house. Now a dog was chained outside the house that barked and snarled in rage. I was no longer welcome in my old home.

I let the years take me back. The wind blew softly, and the warm smells of Texas surrounded me. Charles stirred at my side and smiled, bringing me back to the present.

"See what you came to see?" he asked me. I smiled at him and my gaze took in his concern and my son's slight air of concern. I loved them both. I lovingly tightened my hold on the hand of the fearful ghost child who still stood at my side. She trusted me, and needed me, to love and care for her. I silently reassured her that this trip had been necessary and turned to go.

"Yes," I replied, "I've made a beginning."

CHAPTER TWO
BABY GIRL

At two years of age I could easily stand upright in my crib. Bars of sun glowed in the window and warmed my small bed. I held out pudgy fingers. I loved the pretty light. As I watched varied colored specks of dust dance in the sun I chuckled.

The trees outside the window stood tall and green. Through the blinds I could see their leaves waving in the clear air. The day was bright, and I could hear voices of children racing about at play. I would like to play too, but I am not big enough. I wished Mommy would put my playpen in the green yard. Then I would be allowed to touch the grass. I would be able to watch my big brothers at play. Now, I am not taken outside. I am in my crib and I must take a nap.

I was not tired. Standing upright in my sleepers I looked around the room. What a nice room! The wooden floors were light golden brown, and the sunshine made puddles of gold in front of my bed. Two large windows were covered with blinds that were drawn half closed. In the corner stood a large wooden radio. Crystal buttons marched across the front and it sat tall and rounded on the wooden floor. I loved the radio. It made happy sounds and I knew it as my friend. The radio never shouted meanly to make me cringe and cover my ears. I loved to toddle on the floor and hug its fat middle.

Suddenly, Mommy bustled into the room. I love my Mommy. She has soft hands and a low voice. I love to hug my Mommy. I put out my arms for a hug. Mommy hugged me and scolded in a soft voice. "Shame Chrissy! Mommy told you to take a nap. Lie down and go to sleep like a good girl!" Mommy gently pushed me flat in my crib.

I fidgeted for a few minutes, but finally fell asleep. Suddenly, I was aware of hands touching me. I rolled over to get away from the hands, but I was firmly turned back over.

"Be still," a voice whispered, "be quiet. I won't hurt you. You are my good little girl."

I peeked through squinted eyes. Was that my daddy? I am afraid of Daddy. He screams loud and hits hard with big hands. I do everything my daddy says. I lay very still.

Slowly, Daddy unbuttoned my sleeper. He pulled it down. My legs were cold, and I trembled. Daddy put his big hand on my leg and began to touch me. He pushed his finger inside a secret place. It burned like fire and hurt sharply. I began to cry.

Quick as a flash, Daddy turned me on my tummy. He spanked my bottom with his hand. I screamed as Mommy ran into the room.

"What's wrong?" she cried, "Chrissy should be taking her nap."

"I am spanking her because she won't mind," Daddy said. "You told her to go to sleep. I came into the room and she was playing."

I cried because Daddy said I was bad. I was minding Mommy. I was sleeping. Daddy woke me up and he hurt me with his big hands. Maybe Mommy would make him stop. I wanted Mommy to fix my hurt.

"She's only a baby, Jimmy, don't spank her. She isn't big enough to understand." Mommy said.

"She's big enough to obey. I won't tolerate the children disobeying you!"

Daddy pulled my sleeper back on and gave me a little shake.

"Now go to sleep!" he said harshly.

I sobbed quietly while Mommy and Daddy left the room. I found my yellow blanket and held it tightly. I looked at the radio. I wanted it to make happy sounds and comfort me. Hiccupping, I slowly cried myself to sleep.

CHAPTER THREE
UNCLE JOE

A sunshine day sang outside, and I was four years old. It was cool for it was springtime and the air was soft. I felt happy. Today I was going to play at my cousin Elizabeth's house. Patiently, I sat in my little chair while Mommy braided my long brown hair. I didn't cry when she pulled tangles with the sharp comb. I must be very good to be allowed to play with Elizabeth.

At last Aunt Peg came to pick me up! Elizabeth waited in the car. We sat in the back and chattered all the way to her house. As Aunt Peg pulled up in the driveway Elizabeth and I leaped shouting from the car. We raced around her house, laughing and playing. Suddenly, I stopped, joyous. Uncle Joe was home! How I loved Uncle Joe. I held up my arms and he swung me high off the ground and twirled me in circles. Dizzy and happy, I held onto him tight.

Uncle Joe was Aunt Peg's husband. He wore a blue uniform and drove a big truck. Uncle Joe kept our butane tank full. He was jolly and happy, and I loved to run and meet him as he hooked the fat hose to the gray butane tank.

Now, as Aunt Peg drove away to go shopping, Uncle Joe set me on the ground. Elizabeth sat down in the shade to play with her dolly. Uncle Joe kept tight hold of my hand.

"Want to go in the house and play with Uncle Joe?" he asked me.

I nodded, pleased. I loved Uncle Joe so much! He never screamed and yelled like Daddy. I wished with all my heart that Uncle Joe could be my own daddy.

Holding my hand Uncle Joe took me into the house. He swung me to his shoulder, and we galloped down the hall. I hung onto him laughing and pretended that he was my daddy. We galloped into the room with the big bed. He bounced me onto the white bedspread, and I lay there chuckling, adoring him with my eyes. Uncle Joe leaned over me and pushed my nose.

"I know a secret," he whispered, "can you keep a secret with Uncle Joe?"

Eagerly, I nodded. I wanted to know the secret.

"You're a sweet girl, a smart girl," Uncle Joe pulled one of my long braids gently. "I know you can keep a secret. I love you, Chrissy, I love you so special! That's our secret, okay?"

I lay on the bed and kicked my feet. "Okay!" I said with a happy smile.

"Now, you can't tell Mommy or Auntie Peg that I love you special," gently, he tickled my tummy. "What's this?" he leaned over and softly kissed my mouth. "Sweet baby lips! Can you kiss Uncle Joe?"

I gave my uncle a smacking kiss on the mouth and hugged him hard. I made Uncle Joe happy.

"What a good girl!" he said, "she loves her Uncle Joe." He put a gentle hand on my leg and began to stoke it. I wiggled in pleasure. I liked the feel of his hand on my bare leg. Uncle Joe pushed my skirt up and rubbed higher. I felt him touch my lacy, white panties. I lay still. This felt good, but strange. But I loved Uncle Joe. He would never hurt me.

Gently, Uncle Joe pulled my panties down. His soft hand kept stroking me, gently. He pulled my panties off and spread my legs apart. I lay on the bed and watched him. I trusted Uncle Joe. We were sharing a secret. Uncle stared hard at my spread legs. He touched a place between my legs, and I felt his fingers open it wide. I squirmed. He kissed that spot between my legs. His tongue licked gentle, wet and warm. I hardly breathed. Strange warm feelings were rolling in my tummy.

"Don't make a sound!" Uncle Joe raised his head and locked my eyes with his. "This is our secret. The door is locked, and Elizabeth cannot come in. She will not know our secret. No one will know that Uncle Joe loves you so special." He lowered his head and licked me some more. I touched his crisp black hair with my little hand. He caught my hand and kissed it. Then he put his mouth between my legs and gulped hard. He sucked me hard. It hurt. I wiggled and whimpered because I did not like it. Tears came into my eyes.

"Sh," Uncle Joe said. He raised me up and sat on the bed beside me. "Look."

He unzipped his pants and reached inside. He pulled out a long, hard thing that had a purple head. "Give me your little hand. That's right! Touch it! Isn't it nice? See, this is our secret. Go on, kiss it! Put your little mouth right on top."

He held my head over his lap while I kissed him there. As he pushed me down, he forced that hard-purple thing into my mouth. I didn't know what to do. I had to open my mouth very wide because it was so big. He kept pushing and pushing. I was choking and crying, but finally, some white, sticky stuff shot out of the purple head. I choked and tried hard not to throw up.

"Sh," Uncle Joe wiped my face with his shirt tail. "See, it's all right. Everything is all right. We have a secret. You have made Uncle Joe very, very happy. Good girl! I'm proud of you, and I know you will keep our secret." He reached for my panties and gently pulled them over my shoes. Setting me on my feet, he pulled them up and straightened my skirt.

"You and Uncle Joe have a secret," he said, squatting on his heels and looking into my eyes. "Remember, don't tell anyone our secret!" Standing up, he once again swung me to his shoulders. I held on tight and laughed to please him. Uncle Joe and I had a secret.

CHAPTER FOUR
LOVE IS MOMMY

The morning air was sweet. The scorching heat of midmorning had yet to burn the early dew off the grass. The birds blended their voices in glorious melody. The flowers called, sweet and wild, filling the air with bright and varied colors. I loved the velvet red of the Indian Paint Brush and I was intent on getting some for Mommy.

Rushing headlong into the tall grass, I paused captivated by purple and blue flowers. Mommy loved these! Pleased, I pulled bunches out of the ground. When I had made a colorful bouquet, I trotted back to the house.

I paid scant attention to the horned toads and lizards as they scuttled across my path. I cast one longing look at the brown toad, which barely missed being trod upon. I could play later with my wild pets. Mommy was waiting for her flowers. I proudly bore them to the bedroom door.

"Look Mommy!" I cried, dancing through the open door. "See what I've brought you!" Mommy turned her head on the pillow. A smile lit her thin, tired face. Her blue eyes were warm with approval.

"Beautiful, Chrissy!" she praised me, "the flowers are just beautiful! Put them on the dresser where I can see them."

"Okay, Mommy. Thank you, Mommy." I put the flowers on the dresser.

"Good girl! Are you watching the little ones?"

"Yes, Mommy. They are outside playing."

"Go back out and make sure they don't get under Grandmother's feet."

"Okay, Mommy." I kissed her and hurried out. Grandmother was sweeping the kitchen floor. I stopped to hug her then raced out into the hot sunshine. Tommy and Tracey, my little brother and sister, were playing in the back yard. I half listened to their happy voices as I watched them. I was thinking about Mommy.

Please, God, I prayed silently. Don't let Mommy go back to that hospital. I was a big girl, five years old, and for as long as I could remember Mommy had been sick. I must work very hard to watch the little ones and help Grandmother in the house because Mommy was not strong. I wanted to do all I could to help Mommy get well.

The Texas sun scorched the clay in the back yard. It poured down hot and burned my skin. I wiped sweat from my face as Tommy pulled my sleeve.

"Please, Chrissy," Tommy begged, "go in." At three, he was a good talker.

"Let's see," I said. I peeked around the corner to see if the old green truck was parked in front of the house. The long driveway was empty, so Daddy wasn't home. I took Tommy and Tracey into the house.

"Grandmother," I explained, "they are so thirsty. It is really hot out there. We need to come in."

"Christine, you know your daddy doesn't want you children in the house," Grandmother said, as she filled plastic cups with water. "You might disturb your Mommy."

"We'll be quiet," I promised her, "and he'll never know." Tommy and Tracey turned on the small television set and sat on the hard, wooden floor to watch cartoons. I tiptoed to the bedroom door, and eased it open to look in. Mommy's eyes met mine and she smiled.

"Come in, Honey," she invited.

I happily snuggled in the big bed. The water cooler hummed, filling the room with cool humid air. I listened to it drip as Anne, my baby sister, tossed restlessly in the crib by Mommy's bed. How happy I was!

"Let me brush your hair, Mommy." I took the wooden brush and moved it through Mommy's hair.

I brushed her hair until she fell asleep. I was falling asleep too when Grandmother appeared at the door, looking anxious.

"Your daddy's home!" she hissed.

Quick as a flash, I slipped off the bed. Hurrying from the room, I scooped up Tommy and Tracey and rushed them into our bedroom at the back of the house. We sat there quietly, waiting as the truck's engine died in the front yard. Daddy was home.

CHAPTER FIVE
FEAR IS DADDY

Later, in the cool of the evening, deep purple shadows touched the grasses, but my eyes did not see all their beauty. I sat on the side of my bed shaking. The turmoil in Mommy's bedroom was mirrored inside me. Her temperature was soaring, and Daddy was taking her to the hospital. I sat, afraid to move. Daddy appeared at the door.

"You damn kids obey your grandmother or I'll make you wish you hadn't been born! Understand?"

"Yes, sir!" My older brothers, Donald and Mitchell, answered in unison. I listened as the old blue car roared to life, and spewed gravel down the long driveway. The house was empty, and inside, I felt empty too.

Twilight fell. I felt alone, empty, and blue. Loneliness filled me, and I drew no comfort from the presence of my brothers and sisters. Mommy had gone away. Her tender love would not surround and protect me from Daddy. How I wanted Mommy! I wanted her to be well and strong. God had not heard my prayers.

"Bedtime," Grandmother called from the kitchen. For a long time, I lay and stared at the lonely tree outside the bedroom window. The television blared softly from the living room, and I heard the clatter of dishes in the kitchen. Grandmother was cleaning up from our hasty supper. Muffled sobs came from the bed Tommy shared with Tracey. I rolled on my stomach and tried to comfort him.

"Want Mommy," he buried his head under the covers. I tried to comfort him as he sobbed himself to sleep. I had fallen into an uneasy sleep, when I was awakened by the slamming of the kitchen door. I heard a rumble of voices in the kitchen. The door banged again, and Grandmother's shoes tapped on the wooden porch. Her car purred to life and we were alone with Daddy.

"Goddamn," he swore loudly, "which one of you goddamn kids lost the key off the alarm clock?"

Silence filled our bedroom. Donald and Mitchell feigned sleep.

"Answer me! Which one of you goddamn kids lost it?"

Screwing up my courage, I called out, "We didn't lose it, Daddy."

"You didn't lose it." Daddy's voice dripped sarcasm. "I'm goddamned crazy, aren't I? The key is gone but nobody took it. Nobody took it, Daddy." His voice was high and thin, mocking me. I began to cry as I listened to his voice go on and on.

"First, you break your mother's health, and then every damn one of you lies. What did I ever do to deserve you?"

I stuffed the sheet into my mouth. If he heard me cry, I would be punished. Daddy's voice rose to a scream.

"One of you goddamn kids come in here and take my socks off!"

I was afraid to move. Finally, I tumbled from bed and crept into his room. Daddy looked at my swollen eyes. His small green eyes and mean mouth made me shiver in fear. Timidly, I knelt to pull his socks off. He kicked at me, and I flinched, dodging his foot.

"You damn kids ought to cry your eyes out! If she dies, it's your fault!" he snarled.

As I crept back to bed, fear stabbed at me. I didn't want Mommy to die! I cried silently in my bed. Tears ran down my face and I sobbed without making a sound. I heard Mitchell sobbing helplessly in his own bed. My big brother Mitchell never cried! I knew that Mommy must be very sick for Mitchell to cry. Later, my heart broke in my chest as I listened to my daddy's sobs rack the night. The world is truly horrible when a strong daddy must cry. I wanted to comfort him, but I was afraid. Worn out from my own crying, I finally fell asleep.

Despite everything, I woke early the next morning. I listened to make sure daddy was asleep. When I was sure I could hear his heavy snores, I slipped from my bed. I tiptoed past the bunk beds, where my older brothers slept, and the little twin bed Tommy and Tracey shared. Easing one foot in front of the other, I made my way to the bathroom, careful not to tread upon any board that might creak. Back in bed after the necessary trip, I heaved a sigh of relief. We were not allowed to go to the bathroom while Daddy was sleeping. Often, I had waited in agony for him to get up, praying I would not have an accident in my bed.

In Daddy's room, the bedsprings creaked. He shuffled into the bathroom and I heard water running. In a moment, he was at our bedroom door. His face was tight with anger.

"Which one of you kids left the water running in the bathroom? Get into the living room! Now!"

I looked at Tommy and Tracey. Their faces were twisted with fear. How I wanted to protect them! Slowly, the five of us filed into the living room, all traces of sleep wiped from our eyes. Daddy had his big belt looped in his hand.

"Bend over!" he ordered.

He moved toward Donald. My eyes were shut, but I could hear him beating my brother. The sound was like ice cracking in the winter. As Donald screamed, my mind flashed to an incident two weeks prior.

Daddy had seen Donald hit me. Without a word, he grabbed Donald's arm and threw him heavily into the living room.

Forcing Donald to pull off his pants, and then his underwear, he made us watch as he swung his big belt against Donald's naked buttocks. Donald's bottom clenched under the blows and trembling with pain, he screamed. I couldn't stand to watch, and I hid my face against Mommy's waist. Guilt washed over me. It was my fault Daddy was whipping him.

Now, as I came back to the present, I trembled. My turn was next. I hardened myself for the pain, but there was no way to be prepared. It wrapped around my legs like fire, traveled up my back, and took my breath away. I howled for mercy. Again, and again, the fire licked over me.

The noise woke Anne in Mommy's room and she cried. I ran to pick her up. Daddy was putting on his belt, preparing to leave for work. Grandmother was coming to stay with us. Daddy gave us a warning as he went out the door.

"If any of you cry to your grandmother, I'll make you wish you hadn't been born. Got it? I won't have her upsetting your mother."

"Yes, Daddy, sir," I said, I wouldn't dare tell Grandmother. Somehow, the days and weeks would go by until Mommy came home from the hospital. Surely, once Mommy was home, we would be safe from Daddy. Mommy would take care of everything.

CHAPTER SIX
THE SPANKING

Golden sunbeams scattered across the yellow counter and warmed the yellow wall phone. The breeze wafted warmly through the open screen door. The kitchen felt big, open, roomy and friendly. The stainless-steel double sink was empty of dirty dishes and the big white refrigerator was waiting to be filled with food. In the pasture, brown, white, and spotted cows grazed with contentment. I was happy as I played with my favorite doll.

Mommy was finally home from the hospital. She was feeling so well, that she had gone shopping. I was waiting for her to come home, because she was bringing me some gum!

I stuck a plastic thermometer in my doll, Suzanne's, mouth. Just as I was putting her to bed, the phone rang I ran to pick it up. Feeling very important, I spoke in my grown-up voice.

"Hello, Anderson residence,"

"Hi, Chrissy," Mommy's voice came over the wire.

"Hi, Mommy!"

"Where's Daddy?"

"Oh! He's cutting the yard." I traced circles on the yellow counter, "Do you want him?"

"Well, no, don't bother him. What's he doing?"

"He's riding on the big lawn mower."

"Okay. Be a good girl. I'll see you when I get home."

"Bye, Mommy." I turned to Suzanne, "Now be a good girl. Mommy will be home soon with your gum!"

I was soon absorbed in my game. Every now and then, I ran to look down the long driveway. I was impatient for my gum! After a long time, I saw Mommy's blue car coming down the road. Finally! She was bringing the good food home to put in the refrigerator. I watched as Daddy turned the big riding mower toward the house. Probably he was happy to see Mommy come home.

The car ground to a halt by the front door. Stopping the noisy mower, Daddy jumped off and ran toward Mommy, waving his arms. I couldn't hear what he was saying, but I could see that he was angry. He grabbed Mommy's arm and shoved his face within inches of hers. Mommy pulled her arm free and pointed toward the house.

My heart pounded. I squeezed Suzanne very tight. Holding her gave me comfort. I searched my memory. Had I done something wrong? My throat was dry as I tried to swallow a huge lump of fear. Suddenly, Daddy tore through the door and grabbed my arm.

"Goddamn you!" he screamed, dragging me into the bathroom. "You goddamn kid! Why didn't you tell me your mother called? I've been out of my head with worry." He began to slap me. "You knew I was going to call the police! What the hell is the matter with you? Don't you have any common sense? I'll teach you to open your goddamn mouth!" He jerked my jeans off and pulled down my panties. When my bottom was bare, he threw me across the bathtub and grabbed a wooden paddle he kept for stirring paint.

"I'll beat your ass!" he screamed, as he began to hit me. I twisted away from the blows as best as I could.

"You goddamn worthless kid!" he screamed.

"Daddy! Daddy!" I was hiccupping in my effort to tell him something. "I didn't know! Mommy told me not to bother you! Stop Daddy, please stop! Mommy said not to bother you!"

Daddy stopped beating me and went into the kitchen to confront Mommy.

"Did you tell this child not to bother me?"

"I didn't tell her that!" Mommy sounded horrified.

Daddy returned to the bathroom and resumed the punishment. My legs and back hurt so terribly I thought I would faint from the pain. Daddy seemed angrier than ever.

"Never, never, lie to me again, Christine!" he said. "I'll teach you to tell the truth if it kills you." He hit me several more times and finally left me crumpled, sobbing on the bathroom floor.

Much later, I crept from the bathroom to the bedroom. Sitting carefully on my bed, I tried to understand my crime. I really hadn't known Daddy was worried about Mommy. I walked painfully to the hallway and look at my mother. She was rushing through bags, putting groceries in the cabinets. She glanced up from her task.

"Does your bottom hurt?" she asked her blue eyes warm and compassionate.

I looked at her but didn't answer. Holding Suzanne, I walked slowly back into the bedroom.

"Christine! Get out here and watch these kids!" Daddy yelled.

I brushed the tears from my face and hurried as quickly as I could out the back door. There was no private time for crying.

CHAPTER SEVEN
POLLY

There were four of us. The oldest three made a tight knit group, and the fourth was a tag-a-long little boy. Donald, Mitchell, and I wanted to leave him at home with our baby sisters, but Mommy said we must bring Tommy along. Donald as the oldest was a tall, skinny, ten-year-old, very wiry and strong. His sandy crew cut stood at attention on his erect, round head. Blue eyes alert and full lips sucked inward, he considered where to begin. Clutching a coffee can tightly in his dirty right hand; he scanned the sticker bushes for the choicest blackberries.

Yellow jackets buzzed thickly in the open flowers. Mitchell carefully brushed them away as he began picking the ripe berries. He had already spied out the thickest clusters. A sturdy eight-year-old who was intent on his work, Mitchell wasted no words. Today he wants to pick enough berries for Grandmother to bake cobbler.

Today, I am feeling somewhat cross. Usually, my two older brothers and I are just like the three musketeers, but today they are making me watch Tommy, who is too little to pick for very long. I am mad, because Mommy would not keep him at home. My short brown hair clung to my forehead, and my striped shirt was sticky with sweat.

Tommy sat in the grass and looked up at me with big, green, four-year-old eyes. His blond hair fell into his eyes. Crying, he held up his foot for me to see.

"Stickers, Chrissy!" he wailed.

Sighing, I grasped his foot. "Your thongs are full of stickers, Tommy!" I scolded, "Why can't you be more careful?"

"I, sorry," Tommy whimpered, lower lip protruding.

Guilty because I scolded him, I carefully removed several spiky thongs from his dirty foot. That's all right, Tommy," I soothed him, "here, take your jar. Can you pick these big berries on this bush? Watch out for bees."

"I pick!" Beaming, Tommy took his little jar and began to fill it with berries. I watched for a minute, convinced he would eat more than he could pick.

Selecting a bush close to Tommy, I went to work. Bees hummed close by, singing in the early summer stillness. Mockingbirds called to one another in the trees and a small green lizard slithered over my foot. I was not afraid of lizards, and we had been taught to look out for snakes. It was a deliciously cool morning, and the sun shone gently warm. My heart began to feel content. I ate some of the sweet berries. They slid sweetly down my throat and stained my mouth with purple juice. Here among the berries, Daddy seemed far, far, away. Mommy was home, and the world felt right. I picked as fast as I could. I wanted to keep up with Mitchell and Donald.

The morning passed quickly. When we got tired of picking, we sat in the shade and discussed our plans for the afternoon.

"Let's go to the woods!" Donald suggested.

I was pleased with the idea. I loved the woods. They were cool and green in the hot summer sun. We could look for lizards and horned toads. We might even see a mother fox hiding in a den with her babies. We could climb the trees and swing out on the branches. I hoped Mommy would let me go. Maybe we could even play pioneers and build a hut from fallen tree limbs. Full of plans for the afternoon, we gathered our berries and headed for the house.

"Go this way!" Donald shouted.

"Beat you home!" Mitchell challenged him.

"Wait for me!" I panted from behind, dragging Tommy along by his sticky hand.

It was fun, pushing our way through the tall grass that grew around the edge of our property. We were running, and I began to play, I was an explorer in a new world. The danger of wild animals was all around. Suddenly, a cry from Mitchell broke into my pretend game.

"Polly! It's Polly!" Mitchell was sobbing.

"What's wrong? What is it?" I cried, crowding close.

Quickly, we clustered around him. Directly at his feet almost hidden by tall grass, lay his kitty, Polly. Polly was a beautiful kitty with soft black and white fur. She would come quickly, purring when we called her. She was soft, warm, and purring with love.

Now she lay still in the grass, cold and dead. Her little soft body was twisted and hard. Her mouth was open in a silent meow of pain. I felt sick. Clutching our berries, we began to run.

"Mommy! Mommy!" Mitchell screamed.

"Mommy! Mommy!" I echoed him. Ahead of me, Mitchell was running with all his might. I could hear him crying for Mommy. Donald and Tommy were running and crying too.

Mommy met us on the porch. "What's wrong?" she cried.

"Polly's dead! Polly's dead!" we sobbed. Mitchell tried to explain through his tears.

"She's all twisted up and hard. She tried to call for help but nobody came. She died, Mommy! She died!"

Mommy looked at us helplessly. She put her arms around Mitchell and tried to comfort him.

"I'm so sorry, honey, that you kids found her. Maybe she ate some poison that someone put out to kill the rats."

With all my might, I hated the mean person who would poison our precious Polly. I tried to understand why the gentle kitty who loved us must die. I wanted Polly to be alive. Now she was taken away and could never come back. I hurt inside. No new kitty could ever take Polly's place. The beautiful day was spoiled. Even the blackberry cobbler Grandmother baked did not help. I would never forget Polly.

CHAPTER EIGHT
THE BEDROOM

Sitting upright on my bed, I watched the early evening sunlight. It was only six o'clock in the evening and the daylight was not ready to go to bed. I was resentful. There were so many things I could be doing out there in the balmy, summer evening! My favorite tree, the one that often gave me comfort, rustled an invitation just outside the dirty glass window. Warm light streamed through that window, highlighting every smudge and dirty fingerprint. Not even a shade covered its openness.

Our bedroom was alive with whispers. Although it was so early on Saturday evening, all six of us had been sent to bed. Daddy must leave for his job at the newspaper in the middle of the night. He would make sure that the paper boys made all the early, Sunday morning newspaper deliveries. Daddy could not sleep unless we were all in bed. We must be perfectly quiet. If he heard us make even a little noise, he would wake up and punish us.

I sighed. I was bored. I was not sleepy this early at night! The sun was still shining, and the early evening breezes called me to come and play. Frustrated, I flopped on my stomach, and investigated the two bunk beds on my left. Donald was hanging over the top bunk deep in conversation with Mitchell. I wondered what they were talking about.

Our bedroom was small and crowded. Wedged between Donald and Mitchell's bunk beds to the left, and Anne's crib on the right, my small bed felt confining. At the head of my bed just inside the door, Tommy and Tracey played quietly in their own bed.

I ran my fingers restlessly over the wooden headboard on my bed. I explored all the marks my teeth had bitten into the soft wood. I hoped Daddy would not see the marks, he would probably punish me. I sunk my teeth into the headboard one more time and tasted the wood. I felt some of my frustration slip away. I heard a slight scuffling noise and I rolled over to watch Donald and Mitchell.

Mitchell was out of bed and sitting Indian style on the wooden floor. He rolled his covers into a ball and tossed them to Donald. Donald grabbed for the ball of sheets and blankets but missed, and it bounced against the exposed insulation, hanging from the unfinished wall.

"Be careful!" Mitchell hissed, "I don't want to itch all night!"

Giggling softly, Donald grabbed the makeshift ball. He was very quiet, in order not to wake Daddy. He and Mitchell were adept at playing silent games.

"Throw it to me!" I whispered. Donald tossed it to me, and I threw it to Tommy. Soon we had a rollicking, if silent game of catch going.

Slowly, the room grew darker. Shadows reached into the window and the moon rose full, glowing with yellow light. I was having so much fun, playing in the dark and giggling!

"Throw it here," Donald ordered. He stretched tall on his bunk and tossed the ball to Tommy.

"Here Chrissy!" Tommy threw the ball to me.

I heaved it over the side of Anne's crib. She clapped her hands with the fun. Suddenly, the room grew very still. I was still giggling uncontrollably when the light snapped on. As I looked up, the smile faded slowly from my face. Daddy stood, tall and angry in the door. He was frowning meanly, and his heavy belt was looped in his hand.

"I told you goddamn kids to be quiet!" He advanced on me. "Roll over!" he snarled. Holding me down with one hand, he whipped my bottom with his heavy belt. I screamed and twisted as the heavy leather bit my skin. Daddy crushed my face into the pillow. I couldn't breathe and strangled on my cries.

"Shut up!" Daddy screamed. I gulped back my cries as he beat us, one by one. Even little Anne was hit. She turned her face to the wall and sobbed. I put my hand into the crib and held her hand tightly. I offered her what comfort I could.

Finished at last, Daddy lumbered from the room. From their bedroom, I could hear him talking to Mommy.

"Those goddamn kids were playing! Every goddamn one of them." He bit the words off in anger. "None of them were sleeping. They could care goddamn less if I have to get up at two in the morning to feed their goddamn bellies!"

"Not Christine!" I heard Mommy cry, "She's always so good!"

"Especially, Christine," Daddy replied, "I caught her in the goddamn act."

I buried my head in my hands and sobbed. Mommy was disappointed in me. I was not her good girl.

CHAPTER NINE
FIRST GRADE

The long, hot days of August shimmered over the dry countryside. The once green grass was now burned, brown stubble. The promise of fall was in the air, but the sultry heat made it seem a long way off. The promise of change was in the air, too.

Early one morning as the sun struggled over the horizon, I woke with a feeling of anticipation. Butterflies danced in my stomach as I dressed in the sticky heat. I smoothed my new, navy blue school uniform and hurriedly swallowed a little breakfast. Today was the first day of school! I didn't know what to expect but I had looked forward to the first grade for a long time. Finally, I was going to join my big brothers, and become a school kid.

Holding Mommy's hand, I walked bravely into the first-grade classroom. A tall lady stood at the blackboard. She was dressed in black from head to toe. Only her face, framed in a little white square, was visible. Mommy whispered that I must call this strange lady, 'Sister'.

Mommy gave me a quick kiss and turned to leave. For a moment, I clung to her in fear. The tall lady, with her eyes fixed on me, pointed to an empty chair. I took the seat and my eyes explored the classroom. Bright pictures danced on either side of the blackboard. Tall ABCs marched overhead. A lot of children were sitting around me, but nobody whispered.

"Christine Anderson!" I jumped to my feet. The tall lady wanted me!

"Yes, ma'am," I answered politely, just like I did at home.

"Don't call me ma'am, call me Sister!" The lady said severely.

"Yes, Sister," I said softly, I had forgotten Mommy's instructions.

"Come up here!"

"Yes, Sister!" I hurried to the front of the room. Sister called more names and other children joined me. I watched them quietly as we lined up. About fifteen of us left the big classroom and marched down a long corridor. Finally, we stopped in front of a tiny classroom. As we filed in, I noticed bigger children already seated in the room.

A lady with dark hair and kind brown eyes showed us where to sit. As we noisily found our seats, she introduced herself.

"I am Mrs. Riley," she said, "and this is a split classroom. The first graders will sit on my right, and the second graders are seated on the left. I have taped your names to the front of your seats."

Interested, I looked at the combination of shapes that formed my name. It would be good to know how to read them. Mrs. Riley circulated among us, smelling sweetly of perfume. She passed me a pencil and a piece of paper. When she had returned to the front, she instructed us to copy our names. I put the pencil to the paper and tried to form the curved letter that began my name. My hand would not obey me! Frantically, I erased the messy scrawl that dribbled from my pencil. Again, and again I tried to write. My paper became blurred and black, full of messy holes from erasing. I tried to hide the holes with my arm, curving it around the paper. Mrs. Riley walked among the desks, inspecting the work. When I felt her approaching mine, my heart hammered in fear. She bent her head to look at my messy paper. There was a moment of total silence. The paper was wrenched from beneath my arm.

"Young lady, I thought I told you to write your name!"

I burst into tears of fright. "I tried and tried," I stuttered.

Immediately, Mrs. Riley put her arms around me. "There, there," she soothed, "big girls in the first grade don't cry! Here, give me your hand." Deftly and swiftly, she formed my name on the paper.

I was captivated! How I loved Mrs. Riley! She was kind and good. Immediately, I loved ABCs, numbers, and learning. I began to know Anne, David, and Timmy, the playful children in my first-grade reader. As I began to feel secure in the first grade, I believed I would love school.

My first attempts at friendship did not go well.

"HI!" I said brightly to the little girl sitting next to me, "Will you be my friend?"

"No!" she said roundly. "I don't like you!"

I tried to make friends with some of the other little girls, but I had better luck with the boys. One of them liked to sit next to me in school assemblies. He brought me cake, cookies, and even a dime one day!

St. George School in Ft. Worth, Texas, was its own world, full of rites and rituals. It made me feel so safe! There were the nuns, mysterious and garbed in black. Whenever Sister entered the room, we had to stand and salute her.

"Praise be to Jesus Christ! Good morning Sister!" we would chant in unison. No matter how many times Sister entered the room, we repeated the ritual.

Then, there were the smells. Good cooking smells wafted from the cafeteria and made my stomach rumble in hunger. There was the dry, dusty smell of chalk and the wet smell of the freshly cleaned blackboard. There was the lovely rubber smell of my pink eraser and the freshly sharpened smell of new pencils. I felt happy and safe, sniffing the wonderful smells of my school world.

Mrs. Riley taught us catechism, and we learned about the wonderful Son of God, called Jesus Christ. I learned a lot about Mary. She was the mother of God and had a very important job. I knew that the sisters were called the brides of Christ. That kept them very busy and they could never have an earthly husband, or children of their own. They lived on the school grounds in a place called "The Convent." I was fascinated with the sisters and I wondered if they slept in all their long black clothes.

Mrs. Riley taught us about hell, and a place called purgatory. I shivered when I thought about going to either place when I died. There were big sins called mortal sins and small sins called venial sins. Purgatory was a place where sinners went after death to burn all the venial sins off their souls. There was also a place known as limbo where babies who died without being baptized went to live. It was sad about the babies because they could never see God. A person could always get out of purgatory and live with God in heaven, but hell and limbo lasted forever.

Mrs. Riley also taught us about heaven. It sounded like a wonderful place. Only good people went there. Everyone else had to go to purgatory first. Mary was very good. She lived in heaven, praying for all of us poor sinners here on earth.

Busy as I was learning all these things in school, I was busy at home too. I was almost seven years old, old enough to help with cooking breakfast. I got up early and put the big coffee pot on the stove. I learned how to cook oatmeal and bake canned biscuits. Every day after school I watched the younger children. At night after doing my homework, I gave them a bath and put them to bed. Tommy, Tracey, and Anne were my special responsibility.

I was not allowed to make friends with the children who lived near us. Daddy considered these children to be, "poor white trash." Our school was twenty miles from where we lived. The school bus brought us about eight miles from home and left us at the bus stop. Daddy picked us up and took us the rest of the way home. Sometimes, Granddaddy picked us up or, if she were feeling well, Mommy did. All in all, it took us about an hour and a half to get home.

CHAPTER TEN
SECOND GRADE THE LIE

I wiggled in my seat. The class was attentive as all the eyes watched Sister Grace. I waited to see who she would call next. I willed myself invisible as her sharp eyes swept the room.

"Christine Anderson!" she called, pinning me with her black eyes.

Slowly, I rose from my seat and with dragging steps walked to the front of the room. Karen and Michael were already waiting by the number aide.

"Who wants to be secretary?" Sister asked.

Immediately, I waved my hand. "Me!" I said loudly.

"Michael will be secretary," Sister said. "Now, who wants to operate the number aide?"

"Me!" I shouted hopefully.

"Karen will move the beads," Sister said.

My heart sank. Michael got to write the numbers on the board. Karen got to move the beads that represented units, five's and tens on the plastic number aide. I would have to be team leader and work the problem out. I was afraid.

Sister wrote the problem on the board. I stared at it. Two rows of white numbers stared back. Everything I knew about addition flew out of my head. I swallowed as sweat prickled under my arms. Feeling slow and stupid, I fumbled at the problem.

"Seven plus nine equals nineteen," I mumbled. "Secretary, write down nine and carry the one."

"I am writing nine on the board," Michael began.

"No! No! No!" Sister interrupted. "Michael, don't write that down! Christine, as usual is wrong! No wonder she wanted to be secretary; it hurts her to think! What do seven and nine equal, Miss?"

Uncertainly, I look at Sister. I was so afraid of her! My frozen brain refused to cooperate. Silently, I added again.

"Sixteen is the answer," I blurted.

"Well, well. She finally figured it out," Sister sneered. "Let's all give her a hand, class!" Miserably, I worked my way through the rest of the problem as the class applauded. Tears blurred my vision. I couldn't seem to get anything right for Sister Grace.

As the bell rang for lunch, I bundled my books into my desk. I joined the other children in line, and then slipped away as Sister began to march us down the long hallway. I made my way to the girl's bathroom. Slipping inside, I firmly locked the door to the little stall. I could not face the lunchroom this afternoon. I winced as I sat down, and raising my dress, I rubbed the wide purple welts on my legs. Misery surged inside me as I covered my face with my hands and thought about the night before. Daddy had punished me for taking sugar from the sugar bowl without asking.

I knew I shouldn't eat sugar, but I was so hungry for something sweet. I had spilled some grains on the table. Daddy had noticed the mess and begun to question all of us. When he took off his belt, I knew I had to confess.

"I took the sugar, Daddy," I had whispered.

"Come here!" Daddy said. He pulled up my skirt. As the belt had begun to fall, I had cried. I had not known it was stealing to take sugar.

"You're a dirty little thief and a liar," Daddy had said.

Now, I hunched on the edge of the toilet seat and pulled my uniform over my knees, careful not to put pressure on my legs. I was glad to be alone. I could not eat today! I just wasn't hungry. This morning I had been sick all over the bus again, having vomited every day this week. I dreaded seeing the big bus stop for us. I had always been prone to car sickness, but it was worse this year. Riding on the bus every day was an ordeal. None of the kids wanted to sit next to me.

Finally, the bell rang to signal that lunch and recess were over. I heaved a sigh of relief. The day would soon be over, and I could go home.

That evening over hamburger patties, Mommy looked at me in concern.

"Mrs. Larkin called me today."

"She did?" I asked cautiously. Mrs. Larkin was the cook in the school cafeteria.

"Yes, Sweetheart," Mommy said, "she says she hasn't seen you at lunch for several days."

"Oh, she probably just didn't see me. She's really busy," I said hopefully.

Daddy laid down his fork. "What's going on here, Christine?"

I swallowed the lump in my throat and played with my peas. I knew I had to tell the truth.

"I haven't been eating my lunch, Mommy," I said in a small voice.

"You haven't?" Mommy sounded surprised.

I looked at my plate. "No, ma'am."

Daddy stood up. "Why not?" he asked sternly.

I felt trapped. "The Sisters make us eat all our lunch whether we're hungry or not. I just can't eat all my lunch." I said in a rush.

"Where do you go during lunch, Chrissy? What do you do?" Mommy asked.

"I hide in the bathroom," I admitted.

"We'll see about this," Daddy said. "I don't like the idea of the nuns forcing my kids to eat. I'm going to do something about this."

"Why does Sister make you eat all the food, Chrissy?"

"She says there are too many starving pagan babies in wild countries to waste food," I answered truthfully.

The next morning, I left for school clutching a long-typewritten letter. Daddy had addressed it to Sister Grace. I placed it in her thin white hand as we lined up for morning mass. As the choir lifted their voice in "Ave Maria," I wondered about the note's contents. I could not concentrate as the priest lifted the host for us to reverence. All I could see was the note clutched in Sister's folded hands. On the way back to class, Sister caught me by the arm.

"Why did you tell your father I force you to eat all your lunch?" her face was set in angry lines and her black eyes glittered.

"I didn't tell him that!" I cried, backing away from her in fear.

Sister caught me by both arms and shook me soundly. I could hardly hear her words through the fear ringing in my ears.

"I will have a conversation with your parents this evening, Miss!"

"Yes, Sister," I stuttered.

All through that long, miserable day I tried to concentrate on my work. Sister wrote numbers on the board for us to copy. I squinted my eyes from my seat in the middle of the room and copied them on my paper.

"What are you doing, Christine?" Sister asked.

"I'm copying the numbers on my paper, Sister," I replied and returned to my work.

"Christine Anderson!" Sister's voice was furious.

I jumped in my seat. "Yes, Sister!"

"Come up here," her voice was suddenly silky. I hurried to the front of the room.

"Hold out your hands," Sister ordered. I held them out. In unbelieving horror, I watched as Sister took her long ruler and hit my fingers. The stinging pain brought tears to my eyes.

"Now, return to your seat and pay attention!"

"Yes, Sister," I said. I blinked back tears as I heard snickers from the children around me. My face burned like fire. Girls never got spanked in Sister Grace's class. I was the first. I tried to understand why Sister had spanked my hands. I was only doing what she told me to do. Numb, I sat in my seat and waited for the end of the day.

At home that evening I told Mommy and Daddy about Sister. Mommy shook her head in disbelief.

"She shook you?" she exclaimed. "Chrissy, are you sure?"

"Yes, Ma'am! Honest!" I stated emphatically.

"Give Sister a call, Mercy," Daddy said.

Mommy called Sister. She talked for a long time while I did the dishes. As I was bathing Tommy, Tracey, and Anne, she came to the bathroom door.

"Daddy and I want to talk to you when you're through."

"Yes, ma'am."

I tucked the little ones into bed and dragged myself into the living room. My bones ached with fatigue. Mommy and Daddy waited on the couch.

"Chrissy, I'm afraid that Sister said she never touched you." Mommy said. "She also said she has never forced you to eat all your lunch."

"But she did shake me!" I cried.

Daddy shook his head. "A nun wouldn't lie, Christine. I don't know why you thought you had to make up this story."

"Maybe, you only think she shook you," Mommy offered. "Maybe, you misunderstood her."

"Daddy, I'm not lying!" I cried. "She did shake me and the Sisters always, make us eat all our lunch!"

Mommy sighed, "You've told us so many lies we don't know when to believe you. Sister would not lie."

I looked at my Mommy and my Daddy. What was the use? Everything was just too hard. All grown-up people were against me. They could not be trusted. I wanted to cry but I didn't. Tears were no use. Tears didn't change anything. I would tell them what they wanted to hear.

"Maybe she didn't shake me," I said grimly. "But the Sisters do make us eat all our lunch."

Mommy's face was sad. "Why do you tell us these lies, Chrissy?"

"I don't know, Mommy."

"Tomorrow, you will apologize to Sister." Daddy said.

"Yes, sir."

The next day in school I cringed when Sister passed test papers back to the class. As she handed me a paper marked with a big red "D" I forced a sick grin on my face. I might as well get it over with, I thought.

"I'm sorry, Sister," I whispered.

"I hope you didn't tell your parents any more lies?"

Looking into Sister's eyes and reading victory there, I said quietly, "No, Sister, no more lies."

CHAPTER ELEVEN
A FRIEND

Wild with impatience, I swung on the thick post at the end of the driveway. Today I was going to Theresa's house! Theresa was my very best friend. Having a best friend was the most wonderful thing that had ever happened to me. Most of the girls at school did not like me at all. Once, much to my pain and embarrassment, the fourth-grade girls had formed a hate club against me. They thought I was strange because I was not allowed to do things after school. They made fun of my scuffed shoes and my frayed sweater. Theresa was different. Finally, I had someone to walk with at school, someone to call on the phone, someone to spend the night with.

Finally! Daddy's new red truck was coming down the road. Now, we could leave. As he pulled up beside me, Daddy looked stern.

"Are you sure all your work is done?" he asked.

"Yes, sir!" I was positive. Clambering into the front seat, I did one more mental check. I had swept the kitchen floor, washed the dishes, and cleaned the bedroom, neatly smoothing all the covers on the beds. I could not think of a single reason why I should not spend the day with Theresa.

The sun poured down hot. As we stopped in front of Theresa's house, I could hear the birds singing. Happily, I waved goodbye to Daddy as Theresa burst out the door to greet me.

"Be sure you're good!" Daddy called as he sped away.

"Hi!" Theresa shouted joyfully.

"Hello!" I shouted back. Together we skipped around the walk to her swing set in the back yard. Chattering and swinging, we made plans on how to spend the golden day before us.

Theresa was a sensible girl. Like me, she didn't have time for stupid boy talk. She had one older brother, to whom neither one of us paid any attention. We had a wonderful time exploring the trees behind her house, scouting for foxes and bears, and pretending to be pioneers bringing home game from the day's hunting.

"Indians!" Theresa screamed.

"Where?" I shouted. I cocked my make-believe rifle. Nothing could harm us while I guarded the cabin.

"Quick! Run for the cabin!" Theresa called.

I broke for the trees running as hard as I could. I fell on the ground, and Theresa collapsed in giggles on top of me. We rolled over and over until we were both covered with leaves.

Later, we sat in Theresa's room and pulled leaves out of our hair. When we were tidy, Theresa's daddy was going to drive us to the pet shop.

Wonderful! There were beautiful fish to see. Some were orange with black stripes, and some were black with no stripes. Mice and hamsters ran on squeaky little wheels. Kittens and puppies tumbled together, and big green birds squawked overhead.

I couldn't believe my eyes. When Theresa's daddy bought me a little goldfish of my very own, I jumped for joy, and then proudly carried it out of the store in its own little bowl. We made one more stop at the toy store where he bought Theresa a jingle toy. Then, we headed for home where Theresa's mother made us a good dinner of steak and mashed potatoes. Her daddy made me roll with laughter as I listened to the silly jokes he told. After dinner, he caught Theresa around the middle and gave her a big hug. I watched in wonder. My daddy never hugged me like that.

"Grr," Theresa's daddy growled, dropping on all fours, "I'm a bear and I love tender little girls."

"Oh no, oh no," shrilled Theresa. We ran screaming as he chased us around the room, growling all the time. As he grabbed Theresa, I became aware of the insistent honking of a car horn. Daddy was here to pick me up! I ran to get my little fish as Theresa's daddy went out front to talk to Daddy.

"We enjoyed having your little daughter," he was saying as I came out, "she is a good little girl. We are glad for her to be friends with Theresa."

"Thank you," Daddy said, "kids can make you proud sometimes, can't they?" He shook hands with Theresa's daddy before we drove away.

"Look at my fish, Daddy." I said, "I'm going to name him Jimmy, after you!"

Daddy looked at Jimmy and his hazel eyes narrowed, "Did you beg for that fish?"

"Oh, no Daddy, sir!"

"You better not. I won't have any of you kids begging."

"Yes, sir."

"The minute you get home you go get the little ones and bathe them for school tomorrow. Your mother's been watching them while you were off, playing. You're selfish Christine, you should have stayed home. You know she isn't well."

"Yes, sir. You said I could go, Daddy!"

"I said you could go as long as your goddamn work was done! You whined and begged enough to go. You made your mother feel so guilty she had to say yes!"

"Yes, sir."

"And, I want the kitchen floor scrubbed. It sticks to my goddamn shoes whenever I walk across it."

"Yes, sir."

"Yes, sir! Are those the only goddamn words you know?"

"I'm sorry, Daddy."

"You should be!"

The beautiful golden day faded in my mind. At home, a pile of dishes filled the sink. Flies buzzed around the dirty pots on the stove. Grimly, I attacked the work, bathed my brother and sisters, and tumbled into bed. Lying there, I wondered in my heart if I was meant to have fun. Why couldn't my daddy be like Theresa's daddy? Her daddy didn't call her selfish. Her daddy let her play. Why was my life so hard? When, if ever, would the pain stop? When?

CHAPTER TWELVE
PAIN

It was a glorious day. The sun burst through the clouds with stunning radiance. The blue, blue, sky made what was taking place in the yard seem all the more horrible.

Two people, locked in combat, stood in the yard.

One was tall, strong and heavy, the other smaller, thinner, and defenseless looking. The smaller figure was crying, as he tried manfully to defend himself. I closed my eyes, unable to bear the sight. Daddy was punishing Donald.

Donald was almost five years older than I was. He was a bully, and most of the time, I almost hated him. He beat on me constantly. I often had purple bruises on my arms after he hit me. For some reason of his own, I knew that Daddy hated Donald. He punished him almost every day. He called him names and made fun of his looks. Today Daddy was beating Donald with his fists. I closed my eyes to the sight, but I couldn't close my ears to the sound.

Splat! Daddy's fist hit Donald's mouth and spurting blood, Donald fell on the ground. Sobbing, Donald struggled to his feet and swung at Daddy.

"Come on! Stupid kid! Worthless! Think you can hit me? Come on goddamn you! Just try!" Daddy's voice dripped with contempt, as a powerful swing of his arm knocked Donald to the ground again. Once more Donald struggled to his feet.

"Stop, it! Jimmy, please stop!" Mommy pleaded desperately.

"Thud!" The powerful fist knocked him down again.

"Stop, Daddy, please! I'm sorry, I'm sorry," Donald cried through broken lips.

Inside my head, the rage grew and grew. It swelled until it was big, black, and terribly ugly. "I hate you!" I screamed it in my head at Daddy. "I hate you! I wish you would go away and never come back. I hate you! I wish you were dead." Trembling with the rage, I ran into the house. I hate this house; I thought wildly, I hate being ten years old! I want to be eighteen, and old enough to leave forever! I ran to the bedroom and jumped on my bed. Lying there, I beat my fists on the bed and bit the pillow, crying and screaming silently with all my might. I didn't dare let Daddy see my anger.

The screen door slammed as Daddy, Mommy, and Donald came inside. Donald was crying. He ran into our room and stood over my bed, his chest heaving. I looked at his battered face as the blood dripped from his lip and spotted my pillow.

"Does it hurt much?" I asked softly.

In answer, he clenched his fist and slammed it into my stomach. I doubled up, crying out in pain.

"What was that?" Immediately, Daddy stood at the door.

God, I thought to myself, does he just stand around, waiting for us to mess up?

"Nothing, Daddy," I muttered through clenched teeth.

"I said, what was that! I want the truth, Christine!"

"Daddy, I only bumped my arm," I lied.

"Sure, you did, goddamn little liar. Can't you and your brother get along? You two are always fighting! Well, I've got the answer to that!" He stomped from the room.

Oh, no, I thought, what is he going to do to me? Suddenly, Mommy ran into the room. She looked worried and afraid.

"Chrissy! Please don't get your brother in trouble," she pleaded, "he's been hurt enough for one day. Tell Daddy it's your fault! He's easier on you than on your brother."

"Mommy, I tried to take the blame. I told Daddy I bumped my arm. He just didn't believe me." I said, feeling miserable. Now, Mommy would be mad at me.

Daddy strode through the door. In his hand was a length of heavy twine about five feet long.

"Come here!"

"Yes, sir," I said, believing he was going to beat me with it. Daddy tied the twine securely around my waist.

"Come here, Donald," he ordered.

Reluctantly, my brother came forward. Daddy tied the other end around his waist.

"Now!" he declared happily. "Where one goes, the other goes. We'll see if this puts an end to the bickering."

I looked at my brother who shrugged his shoulders and headed out the bedroom door. He walked so fast I had to run behind him to keep up.

All that long dreadful day, I followed my brother around. When he went to the bathroom, I sat in the hallway with my head drooping in shame. By evening, my eyes were red and swollen from crying.

"Jimmy, this is crucifying her," Mommy said. "Please untie them."

Daddy untied us at bedtime. I would not look into his eyes. I did not want him to see that I had been crying. That night, as I lay trying to sleep, I made myself a promise. I would always keep a part of myself secret from Daddy. I would ever never ever, let him see how much he hurt me.

CHAPTER THIRTEEN

MY BROTHERS

The piercing cry of a baby tore through the night. Groggily, I rolled on my pillow and tried to shut out the sound. Again, the baby cried, and I struggled to waken. The pitch black outside my bedroom window told me it was the middle of the night. Still, I snuggled in my blankets, warm and relaxed. Maybe this time Mommy would not call me.

"Christine!" The summons came. Groaning inwardly, I struggled from my warm nest. He's her baby, I thought rebelliously. Why can't she take care of him sometimes?

"Christine!" My father's voice was hard.

"Coming!" I struggled into my shower shoes. Making my way to their bedroom, I dropped to the floor by Marvin's baby bed. Inserting one hand through the slats, I began to rub and pat his back. At eight weeks, Marvin still did not sleep through the night.

"Warm his bottle," Mommy murmured.

"Yes, ma'am." I stumbled into the kitchen and removed a plastic bottle from the refrigerator. Moving to the gas stove, I watched the blue flame as the bottle slowly warmed in a pan of water. I shuffled back into the bedroom and cradled Marvin in my arms as he drank. Reflectively, I thought about the school year and his birth.

Fifth grade was not going well. I had appendicitis and had to have an emergency operation. I had actually enjoyed the time I spent in the hospital. The nurses paid a lot of attention to me and were sorry to see me go home. Unfortunately, I had to miss a whole month of school. When I returned, it was to find myself behind the rest of my class. On top of that, I could not run as fast as I could before the operation. Once again, nobody wanted me to play on their team in sports.

Then, Mommy gave birth to Marvin. She could not come home with the baby. She had kidney disease and was gravely ill for six terrible weeks. Once again, we did not know if she would live or die. Once again, I had to leave school. I had to learn how to take care of a baby. I learned how to change and feed him. When he cried, I picked him up and cradled him. He was sweet and I loved him. Now, however, I was back in school and it was hard to get up with him in the middle of the night.

The house was silent. I sat on the floor of my parent's bedroom, and fed my little brother, his small mouth gulping greedily at the bottle I held to his lips. My mind strayed and I began to squirm uncomfortably, remembering an episode with my older brothers. It had happened while Mommy had been in the hospital and Daddy was out visiting her.

"Let's play poker," Donald said.

"Okay," Mitchell and I agreed.

Donald shuffled the cards. The younger kids were in the bedroom sound asleep. My two older brothers and I were alone in the big kitchen.

Donald shuffled the cards. "This is a different kind of poker. Instead of playing for money, we play for clothes. The looser has to take off clothes, one piece at a time," a smile played on his lips, "until they are buck naked!"

I backed away. Even though I was intrigued, I knew we shouldn't play this game. "No! I don't' want to!"

"Come on, Chrissy. Don't be a baby. Do it!" Donald insisted.

"No Donald, it's wrong. I don't want to. If Mommy and Daddy find out, we'll get in trouble."

"Oh, they won't know. Me and Mitchell ain't' gonna tell them. Come on, you know you want to." Donald said.

"Come on, Chrissy," Mitchell added his plea, "we'll have fun. Let's all three agree we won't tell anybody."

I gave in. Once before, Donald had talked me into doing something bad. We climbed into the tree house Daddy had built for us in the back yard. Blocking the door, Donald told me to take off my pants. He spread my legs wide and touched me in a private place. I cried out in sudden pain when he forced his finger inside. I hadn't liked what he was doing. I had felt dirty.

Now, feeling naughty, I joined in the game. Both of my brothers took off their clothes as the cards were played and the game wore on. All I had left on were my panties. We played the last hand and I lost. I didn't want to, but I had to take off my panties. Both my brothers watched me as I eased them down my legs.

"Turn around and show us your bottom," Donald said.

I turned around.

"Bend over."

"No!" Strange feelings were beginning to stir in my lower stomach.

"Look!" Donald pulled out the thing he peed with. I stared at it. It was long and hairy. He began to run around the room, holding it in his hand.

"Vroom, vroom, vroom," he sputtered, making motorcycle noises.

Mitchell and I laughed until we cried. Then Donald came up behind me and bumped his, 'dick' as he called it, against my bare bottom. I grabbed my clothes and ran. Locking myself in the bathroom, I quickly redressed but stayed in the bathroom until Daddy came home.

Now, as Marvin finished his bottle, and I eased him into bed, I was thoughtful. Things were getting very complicated. I was not comfortable around Donald. I felt he wanted to do things to me, things that were wrong, dirty things. I made up my mind to have a talk with Mommy about Donald.

Back in bed, I hugged my nightgown around me, and I winced as one hand brushed my breast. Lately, I had noticed a peculiar change in my breasts. They were swollen and tender. One was slightly larger than the other. I turned over to sleep. It was late and 5:30 would be here before I knew it.

CHAPTER FOURTEEN
CHANGES

Donald tossed the football. I jumped off the porch and grabbed it. I winced with pain as it bounced against my chest. I kept forgetting that my breasts were swollen and tender. I tossed the football back to Donald and climbed onto the porch. I didn't want to play anymore.

Daddy spoke from his chair. "Aren't you playing, Chrissy?" He was in a good mood.

Mommy smiled from her seat. "Maybe, she doesn't want to play with the boys anymore."

I glowed at my parent's interest. "I just don't feel like playing."

Daddy's eyes were on my T-shirt. My small breasts pushed against the soft material, molding it around them. His eyes were small and green, greedy looking. I watched him lick his lips.

"Chrissy is getting big," he said.

I blushed. Arching my back, I strutted across the porch before going inside. It was nice to have attention from Daddy.

Tired from playing so hard, I fell asleep early that night. Awakened suddenly, I sat bolt upright in bed. Donald stood over me. His hand was inside my nightie, stroking my breasts. I shoved his hand away. Something rose up inside me, defiance; I wasn't going to take this from him.

"John Donald Anderson!" I cried. "What are you doing?"

"Shut up!" He hissed.

"Stop that! I'm telling Mommy!"

"I wasn't doing anything," Donald defended himself. "You're dreaming!"

"You were! Keep your hands to yourself!" I cried.

"What's that noise in there?" Daddy's question brought our hissing conversation to an abrupt halt. Ignoring Daddy, Donald ran into the new bedroom Daddy had added onto the house that summer. I lay back down to sleep, but I was wakeful, afraid he would come back.

Early the next morning, I went to find Mommy. White she sorted laundry, I talked to her.

"Mommy, I woke up last night and Donald had his hand on my chest. Under my nightie! He was rubbing my breasts, Mommy."

Mommy sucked air in through her teeth with a soft hiss of sound. "Are you sure you didn't dream it?"

"Mommy! I know the difference between life and a dream! He woke me up."

Mommy nodded. "Calm down," she soothed, "I'll talk to him. Try to understand. Donald hasn't had the normal life of most boys his age. Don't tell your father. He would punish him, and I couldn't stand that. The last time Daddy beat Donald, you remember, he ran away from home. You wouldn't want that to happen again."

"No, Mommy, but I don't want him touching me. I almost hate him, Mommy." I was tempted to tell her about the episode in the tree house, and the episode with strip poker but didn't. I did not want to upset her. Besides, I did not know how she would react.

Once, when I was in the third grade, I had wanted to play with Connie, my girlfriend. Connie lived across the fence, and I was thrilled to find another little girl to play with. She had a little playhouse in the woods, complete with a table, two crates to sit on, and an impressive number of cracked dinner plates.

On that particular day, Mommy had said I could not play, and I was angry.

"You never let me have any fun!" I had shouted, stamping my foot.

Later, Mommy had left in the truck with Daddy. They were gone for a long time. When they finally came home, Mommy was pale. Daddy said he had taken her to the dentist and the dentist had pulled one of her teeth. I got a nasty shock when he turned to me.

"Mommy told me how badly you behaved when she said you could not go to Connie's house. You upset her. For your punishment, go in the bathroom with her, and let her show you her gums! Now!"

I was speechless. I followed Mommy into the bathroom. She opened her mouth and pulled out red, bloody, gauze. Placing her face on my level, she opened her mouth wide and I stared at the bloody hole where her tooth had been. My stomach heaved, and I stumbled from the bathroom, my mind silently screaming, "I'm sorry, Mommy, I'm sorry".

So, now, I did not press her about Donald. I believed she would talk to him. I decided to put the whole thing out of my mind. It was time to enjoy summer vacation. At last, I had time to read all the books I checked out of the public library every Sunday afternoon.

Summertime or not, there was still work to be done. I went to bed each night worn out from a full day. Mommy was still not strong enough to do much in the house, and she spent most of each day in bed. Marvin was walking and he needed a great deal of attention because he was so active. Tracey and Anne were still small enough to need supervision, so between the three of them, I had my hands full.

I was sleeping soundly one night, when I was again awakened by a touch on my breasts. This time when I opened my eyes, Daddy stood over my bed. His hand was under my nightie and he was gently rubbing my breasts. When he saw I was awake, he bent and kissed me on the mouth.

"Good night, Baby," he said tenderly.

I was astonished. What could it mean? Still sleepy, I watched his retreating back.

"Good night, Daddy," I whispered. My mind whirled. I knew it could not be right for Daddy to touch my breasts. Mommy had said I must never let a boy touch me there and Daddy was not a boy, he was my father! It must be wrong for my father to touch me like that. I could go to hell forever for being impure. My heart pounded with fear. Sleepless, I tossed all night.

For the second time that summer, I went to Mommy. I was brushing her hair, as she lay in bed.

"Mommy," I began, "I need to talk to you."

"About what?" Mommy asked sleepily. "Mm, that brushing feels good. Go a little slower."

I obediently slowed the brush strokes. "About Daddy," I said.

"What about him?"

"Mommy," I didn't quite know how to explain, "Mommy, he woke me up last night."

"How come? Did you forget to finish your work?"

"No, ma'am," I squirmed uncomfortably, "he was rubbing my breasts."

"What!"

"He was touching my chest, Mommy. I woke up and found him standing there."

"Are you sure?"

"Yes, Mommy."

"What did he say?"

"He said good night."

"Is that all?"

"Yes, Mommy. I didn't know what to do."

"Well," Mommy said blankly, then again, "well." She shook her head.

"Mommy," I grabbed her in fear, "Mommy, he shouldn't touch me there! I know he shouldn't!" and I burst into tears.

Mommy gathered me into her arms, "Chrissy, sweetheart, don't cry. Don't worry, honey, I'll talk to Daddy."

"Okay," I gulped through my tears. "Thank you, Mommy." I brushed away the tears and felt that I did not have to worry about Daddy anymore. Mommy would take care of everything. That night, I was able to enjoy a good sound sleep.

The next morning, I was happily surprised to find Grandmother at our house when I woke up. When I came into the kitchen to get breakfast, she was sitting at the kitchen table drinking a cup of coffee.

"Good morning, Grandmother!" I ran to give her a kiss. "Why are you here so early?"

Grandmother hugged me. "I have bad news for you. Your daddy had to take your Mommy to the hospital early this morning. She was running a high fever and vomiting."

"Oh, no," I breathed, "where is Daddy now?"

"He went to work."

I was torn. I was troubled that Mommy was back in the hospital, but I was glad Daddy had left for the day. Poor Mommy! She was sick so much of the time. I blamed God. God must be very mean to make her sick so much. The Sister at school had said I must bear the cross of having a sick mother.

Now, I turned to help Grandmother with the work and together we made breakfast.

"I wish that hospital would let me see Mommy," I told Grandmother. "I hate the stupid rule that you have to be fourteen years old."

Grandmother patted my shoulder. "Maybe your Mommy will be home soon."

"I hope so," I sighed.

Later, I was sitting on the living room floor, watching cartoons with the little ones when Daddy walked in.

"What's wrong with you goddamn kids?" he screamed. "How dare you watch television when your mother is sick! Every damn one of you should be on your damn knees praying for her!"

Kids flew everywhere. I hurried into the kitchen where Daddy was banging pots around.

"We'll have sauerkraut and wieners," Daddy announced.

My heart sank. That was the one greasy meal I hated the most. I prepared it, while Daddy took his bath. While he ate, I cleaned the bathtub for him. After his dinner, when he had left to visit Mommy, I fed my brothers and sisters.

"June Bug Gumbo!" Donald said, using his favorite expression for my cooking, "Boy is this stuff nasty!"

"Shut up!" I yelled.

Donald slapped me across the mouth. Crying, I put Tommy, Tracey, Anne, and Marvin to bed early. As they lay in bed playing, I sat in the darkened living room. Their cheerful voices seemed out of place in the gloom. Donald came over to my chair.

"I'm sorry," he said, trying to slip his hand into my blouse, "don't cry."

I pushed him away.

Grabbing my arm, he pulled me to my feet and propelled me into his bedroom. Weakly, I struggled against him. He pushed me into his closet and told me to get on my knees. Although I didn't want to do it, I obeyed him. I felt unable to resist. Donald reached into his pants and pulled out his hard penis. He closed his eyes and shoved it toward my face.

"Suck it!" he ordered, gripping my head.

I tried to shake my head.

"Suck it!" he insisted again, jerking my head. I opened my mouth and took his penis between my lips. In a few minutes, he loosened his hold on my head. I broke away from him. Inside, I felt numb.

"Leave me alone," I said dully.

Donald pulled me from the closet and led me to his bed. Sitting beside me, he stroked my hair. I slumped, uncaring and dull. Donald began talking to me, his voice low and kind.

"You're a real pretty girl, Chrissy, and I love you. Sometimes, I want you to do things for me. Please don't tell Daddy. He would put a neat little bullet hole between my eyes."

"I know," I mumbled, "I won't tell him." Neither of us doubted for a minute that Daddy was capable of such an act of violence. "But I don't like doing that to you! It's wrong! We could go to hell."

"Don't tell Mommy, either. I won't make you do it anymore."

"Promise? Cross your heart and hope to die?" I asked hopefully.

"Cross my heart and hope to die," he agreed.

"Okay," I said relieved, "I won't tell her."

Finally, I was able to go to bed. It had been a long, terrible day. I tried to push Donald out of my mind. I pretended hard that he had never touched me. I felt dirty, unclean and guilty. After a long time, I fell asleep.

Later, as I was sleeping, someone gently shook my shoulder. Daddy knelt over me, his face in the shadow. One hand was under my shirt and the other was in my pants, touching my skin.

"Come into my bedroom, Baby," he said. "I want to talk to you." He rose and walked softly from the room. Fear and dread overwhelmed me. Somehow, I knew my life would never be the same again.

I sat on the edge of Daddy's big bed, trembling, and listening. The electric bulb shed a weak light over the musty smelling bedroom. Daddy was talking and talking . . . his words making circles over my head.

"So, you see, Baby, this is my own special way of loving you. This is something special and precious between the two of us." He drew me tightly into the circle of his arm and stroked my hair. I relaxed against him. It felt so good to have him holding me.

"But, Daddy," I heard myself say, "how can this be right?" From my hiding space within me, I was astonished to hear my words out loud. I thought I had spoken silently.

Daddy continued to stroke my hair. "It's perfectly right. It's my duty as a father to introduce you to sex the right way. Did you know that in ancient societies, teaching a daughter about sex was her father's job? Baby, I tell you it's natural. Modern society has gotten away from the natural order of things."

"But Sister says not to be impure." My voice was muffled against his shoulder. "It's against the church." The words again came from my mouth as I settled deeper inside the secret space within myself.

"I am sure this is good in the eyes of God," Daddy said. "God knows I love you very much. I won't hurt you. I'm sure that many, many fathers do this with their daughters. Don't you understand? I can teach you to enjoy sex the right way! I can teach you about your body, what makes you feel good and what doesn't." He slid his hand gently into my pajama front and softly stroked my breast. "Doesn't this feel good?"

My nipples hardened into little peaks. Against my will I had to admit that it felt very good indeed. I leaned against Daddy. My mind was in turmoil.

"I don't know Daddy. . ." To my dismay I realized I was being drawn out of the secret place within and returning to my "real" self.

"Oh, Baby! I'm giving you a chance to grow up without hang-ups. Forget all the religion crap! That's just something man made up to please himself. Society needs a conscience. There is no God! Or if there is, He doesn't care about what we do."

I was horrified. No God! Daddy shouldn't even say that; I knew he shouldn't.

"Daddy! There is a God! Don't say that!" I cried.

Daddy laughed. "Suit yourself, Baby. If you want to believe in God, go ahead. Just relax and let me show you how special you are. I can love you right. A young kid would just hurt that pretty little body. I can protect you."

He bent his head and kissed my breast. "Doesn't that fee; good?"

"Yes, sir." I admitted.

"You must never ever tell your mother. She couldn't handle it. She doesn't know that incest used to be accepted by society. She has hang-ups. You should feel sorry for her. She will never be as free as you are."

"Yes, sir," I said.

"I mean it, Christine! You can't tell her. It would put her in a loony bin, a nut house. Do you understand me? And you would carry the knowledge to your grave, that you and you alone, were responsible for driving your own mother insane. Do you understand? You can't tell the priest in confession, your teachers or your friends. This is just you and me. Nobody else, period. Understood?"

"Yes, sir." I was miserable. How could I carry all this sin by myself? How could I go to mass, or communion, or look Sister in the face? This is holy hell, I thought, I don't want to do this with Daddy!

"Christine, do you love me?" Daddy demanded to know.

"Oh yes, Daddy!" How very much I loved him, he was my daddy! I wanted to please him, and I wanted him to love me, to be proud of me.

Daddy began to unbutton my pajama top. As the material slid off my shoulders, he ran his hand lightly over my breast. His eyes devoured me as he uncovered me. A shiver ran through my entire body. I was not prepared for how good it felt. Daddy helped me pull of my pajama pants and my underwear and gently urged me to lie across the bed.

I was naked and he gently spread my legs open. He looked at me for a long moment, breathing hard and fast. Using his fingers, he spread my private place open wide and slowly pushed a finger inside of me.

He said, "You are beautiful, and I am preparing you to receive my penis. I will prepare you slowly because I don't want to hurt you. Someday I will put my organ inside of you and you will love it."

I lay still hardly breathing. Part of me felt good. I could feel wetness gathering in the place where Daddy was touching me. I felt guilty because part of me liked what he was doing.

Daddy turned me on my tummy and gently rubbed my bottom. Urging me to my knees he gently spread me from behind as I lay with my face muffled in the pillow.

"I will teach you to enjoy this position too," he whispered softly from behind me. Giving me gentle slaps, he paddled me softly all the while holding his finger inside me. Finally, he pulled it free and helped me to my feet.

"We have plenty of time to learn everything," he said. "Go to bed, Baby. We'll talk more in the morning."

"Yes, sir," I said. Head down, I dragged my tired body down the hall to the bedroom. The relationship between me and Daddy had changed. I couldn't even think about it. I wished we could go back to be the way we used to be. I would rather have Daddy beat me, than touch me this way. Somehow, I knew my life would never be the same again. If I could get some sleep, then maybe I could figure out what to do. Maybe I could run away. If only I could lie down and sleep, and sleep, and sleep. .

CHAPTER FIFTEEN

RAIDS IN THE NIGHT

Sleep was deep and velvet. In my dreams, the night bird sang a haunting tune, a melody both elusive and beautiful. I sang with the bird in a voice sweet and light. I was running through cool meadows when abruptly the night shattered. Hard hands, rough pulling hands, hands that hurt, jerked me from bed. The hands shook me harshly as I tried to focus on the angry voice.

"Stupid!" screamed the voice. "Useless! Worthless! Can't you do anything right? Why must you frustrate me so? Get your ass into the kitchen!"

Confused, I stumbled into the kitchen. Daddy thrust a broom into my hands. Ranting, his voice went on and on. I wanted to cover my ears with my hands.

"Goddamn lazy kid! You're lazy, Christine, nasty! You like things to be dirty, don't you? Look at this floor. It sticks to my goddamn shoes. Sweep it and then I want it scrubbed! And don't use the damn mop. Get on your hands and knees and clean it right!"

I began to sweep the floor. Daddy waved his arms and pointed to the sink where some dishes lay, unwashed.

"I want those dishes washed! Don't you dare go to bed without washing them, if you value your ass! You know how I want this goddamn house kept and, by god, as long as you live under this roof you'll abide by my rules. I better not see things this goddamn nasty again! You got that!"

"Yes, sir," I mumbled, my head bowed.

"What?" he screamed, grabbing my hair and jerking my head upright.

I bit my lip as tears welled in my eyes. "Yes, sir," I whispered again, "I'm sorry, Daddy. It won't happen again."

"It goddamn well better not! I'm the head of this house. You goddamn kids think you're the center of the world. You think you can get away with everything. All you goddamn kids do is take and take! Every goddamn one of you is selfish. Selfish, Christine, you're selfish, do you hear me? All you do is take and take. You goddamn kids will bleed a man dry. You don't have a thought in your head for my comfort or your mother's."

Blindly, I kept sweeping the same spot. "We love you and Mommy," I said softly.

"Words!" Daddy spat. "Words are cheap! Action speaks louder than words. Not one of you knows how to love. All you know how to do is take and take. Well, understand this, young lady, you're not going to ruin my life, and you're not going to ruin your mother's! Do you understand?" Daddy sat heavily in a chair and stuck out his feet. "Take my shoes and socks off," he snarled.

"Yes, sir." I stuck the broom in the corner and knelt to remove his shoes. His feet had sweated and stained the socks a yellow color. Repulsed, I turned my head. Daddy stood up and pushed me aside, lumbering heavily toward the bedroom. When he reached the kitchen door, he turned and fixed me with his small, hazel eyes.

"Don't you go to bed without finishing this floor, Christine!" he warned.

"Yes, Daddy." I wouldn't dare. As he left the room, I sighed. I thought he was finished with pulling me from my bed in the middle of the night. There had been at least six months between this time and the last. Grimly, I filled a bucket with water and attacked the floor.

An hour later, I stood at the kitchen door. The floor sparkled. The dishes shone. I was exhausted but satisfied that everything was clean, and I went to bed.

The persistent ringing of the alarm clock woke me. Bleary-eyed, I checked the time. It was 5:30. I struggled out of bed. My body cried out in weariness, but breakfast had to be made. Half blind with sleep, I shuffled into the kitchen and saw Daddy standing by the stove. Something in his posture made me uneasy. I quietly filled the coffee pot with water and set it on the stove.

"Good morning, Daddy," I said timidly.

"What's that, Christine?" his voice deadly, Daddy pointed accusingly at a bowl of cold oatmeal. Somehow, I had overlooked it in my cleaning the night before.

"I'm sorry, Daddy," was all I could say.

Daddy's hand lashed out and slapped me squarely across the face. "You're not worth the powder to blow you to hell!" he said bitterly.

Feeling numb, I stared at him. My face burned from the slap while his words echoed in my mind. I choked down the hurt. At that moment, I hated him. No matter what I did, I could never please him. It was useless to try. His words rang in my mind, echoing, mocking, "Not worth the powder to blow you to hell."

CHAPTER SIXTEEN
THE CONVENT TRIP

Excitement boiled in my tummy and rose in my throat. I swallowed the lump. I was being allowed to go on a school field trip! The older girls of St. George School were going to spend a whole weekend in a convent. This trip was to be one of the highlights of our Catholic school experience. Every year, the older girls were allowed to go to a convent to see if they had a vocation. I had dreamed of becoming a nun since I was a little girl. I knew I wanted to do something special for God.

I would be spending the night with my friend Casey. Casey's daddy would be taking us to school early Saturday morning. Once there, we would board the bus that would take us to the convent. On the way to Casey's house, I kept pinching myself. I could hardly believe I would be spending the whole weekend away from home.

When I arrived at Casey's house, she and her two sisters Carol and Candy helped me to settle in. They were wonderful to me, and all four of us gathered in Casey's room to gossip. I was almost overcome when they invited me to share in some 'girl talk' with them. I was not used to receiving so much attention.

"What about you, Christine?" Carol asked. "Do you have a boyfriend?"

"Well, sort of," I hedged. I didn't have a boyfriend, but I didn't want to be left out. "There's this neighbor of ours, his name is James." My imagination took hold and I began to fabricate a story. "I guess you could call him my boyfriend."

"Really?" Casey asked, "I heard you like Jeff Morgan."

I was mortified. I had a huge crush on Jeff, but I knew he didn't like me. I was uncomfortable that the other kids in school might have guessed my secret.

"Oh, no," I said, "he's much too immature. James is, well, older. He's in high school."

"Cool." I had caught Candy's attention. "Tell us all about him."

"Well, he's really cute." That much was true. James was our neighbor, but he was Donald's friend, not mine. "He has black hair and blue eyes. He's handsome."

"Where does he live?" This came from Casey.

"Oh, you don't know him." I felt safe because I knew they would never meet James. "He doesn't go to Nolan. He's in public high school."

"Public high school!" Candy was impressed.

"Do you guys do it?" Carol asked, looking wise.

"Do we do what?" I asked, getting nervous.

"You know, fuck!" Candy said, grinning wickedly.

"Candy!" Casey was horrified. "You're not supposed to say that word"

"Shut up!" Candy pushed her off the bed, giggling. "Christine knows what it means!"

"I guess we've made out." I said bravely.

"Really? Cool! What did you do? Come on, tell us!" Carol encouraged me. She smiled at me like I was someone special.

I glowed with the attention. "He kissed me on the mouth!" I boasted.

"Does he feel you up?" Candy wanted to know.

"Uh, huh!" I grew bolder with my false romance.

"Have you ever seen his dick?" Candy asked softly.

I was shocked at her boldness. I stole a glance at Casey. She looked ready to faint. Carol only smiled as they all waited for my answer.

"I've seen it," I boasted, "I've even touched it!"

The girl's eyes grew round with wonder. Encouraged, I pressed my advantage.

"I let him put it down there where my privates are!" I announced triumphantly. I was drunk on their admiration. For the first time I felt that I was fitting into a group. There was a moment of stunned silence.

"You've gone farther than I have," Carol said. Somehow, my news had changed the atmosphere in the room.

"Only once!" I said quickly. I was afraid I had gone too far, and I began to feel guilty about my lies. "He wanted more but I told him no."

The subject was changed, and we talked of other things. I felt safe that they would never find out about my lies. I lived several miles away from school and Daddy never allowed me to bring my friends home. There was no way they would ever meet James.

We giggled and talked through the night even though Casey's daddy told us to be quiet. We were having too much fun to sleep. When I finally drifted off, it seemed only seconds before I was awakened by heavy pounding on the door.

"Rise and shine!" Casey's daddy sang through the door, "it's time for you ladies to get up."

Quickly, I jumped up. After a quick breakfast, we were on our way to school to catch the bus. As we stood in excited bunches chattering, Candy pulled me off to the side.

"I couldn't sleep all night because of what you said about James," she said seriously.

"You couldn't sleep because we were talking," I replied.

"No, really, I'm worried about you."

I listened warily. Candy was older than Casey and often unkind. She liked to tease and torment the younger girls. I did not trust her now.

"Why?" I asked, "You don't know James and you don't know anything about me."

"You're bad to do those things." Candy was completely serious. "It's a mortal sin. If you don't stop it, you're going to hell. I don't know how you can even think of becoming a nun."

I stood stock still. Fear filled my throat like bile. It was true that I had not done those things with James, but Daddy and Donald made me do them all the time. Daddy and Donald made me do worse things.

Suddenly, I remembered the time I had tried to confess to the priest, the episode of strip poker. Trembling in the darkened confessional, I had tried to explain to the priest what had happened.

"What did you do dear?" the priest had asked softly. "I want you to tell me every detail. What were you feeling? Did you have impure thoughts?"

Sweating, I had done my best to confess, but I just couldn't tell him all the awful details. I felt so nasty and impure! I had finally stumbled from the confessional close to tears. I knew I could never talk to a priest again

Now, I listened as Candy continued condemning me. "You're impure, you're a fast girl. You must go to confession," Candy was saying.

Her words sunk in. I was impure. I could not be forgiven, because I could not confess my sins. Guilt chewed at my insides, and I saw myself in hell. There was no hope for me.

I was quiet on the bus ride to the convent. Every time I looked at Candy, she rolled her eyes and looked stern. I felt horrible. I hardly noticed when we arrived. I had been looking forward to this trip but now I could hardly listen to the nun who greeted us. She took us to a dormitory and showed us where we would sleep. There would be lunch and a softball game in the afternoon. I hardly listened as Sister explained the activities of the day. I hardly noticed the hardwood floors, the orderly row of beds, and the soft hissing radiators. The day passed in a blur. The only thing I could see was Candy's condemning face before me.

I tossed and turned all night on the comfortable bed. Ordinarily, the convent atmosphere would have made me feel very safe. I was listless at breakfast and could only nod when Sister asked me to pray about my vocation. She felt God had placed His call upon my life.

Just before the bus left to take us back home, we went to chapel for Sunday mass. I did not dare to take communion. As Candy stumbled past me on the way to communion, she caught me by the arm.

"Pray," she hissed in my ear, "pray for forgiveness!"

I looked at her in misery and nodded dumbly. I slipped to my knees and tried to ask God to forgive me. As Candy made her way to the communion rail, I detected a gleam of victory in her eyes.

"Wait for me after church," she mouthed at me.

Back outside I gulped huge breaths of frosty air. I waited for Candy.

"I'm going to tell your mother," she said seriously as soon as she saw me. To my surprise there were tears in her eyes. My composure crumpled. I felt tears starting to the surface.

"Please, Candy," I begged, "don't tell her, please!" I was desperate. "She isn't strong, and I know she couldn't handle it! Please Candy! I made it all up, anyway. None of it was true."

"I can't let you go to hell," Candy said seriously. She walked away, shaking her head. As I stood there crying, I felt a touch on my arm. Casey stood behind me.

"What's wrong, Christine?" she asked. She looked concerned.

"Oh, Casey," I sobbed, "I'm so upset. Do you remember what we talked about on Friday night?"

Casey looked puzzled, "Oh that!" she said. "I had forgotten all about that."

"Well Candy hasn't." I was sobbing openly now. "I made it up, Casey, all of it. James isn't really my boyfriend. But Candy says she's going to tell my mother everything I said."

"Christine," Casey was earnest in her desire to comfort me. "When does Candy ever see your mother? She's only teasing you. She isn't going to tell your mother anything."

Still crying, I wiped away tears with the back of my hand. I found little comfort in her words. Even if Candy didn't tell Mommy, all the things she said about me were true. I was nasty and impure. I probably would go to hell. My heart was full of pain, and a dark cloud enclosed me. I could no longer feel close to God. Going to mass was a farce. I was going to hell. I would live my life and try not to ever think about God. God would not help me. God did not even want me. I would no longer dream of being a nun.

I was a phony. The dark cloud that covered me was full of lies, and those lies were me. I couldn't bear it. But I must bear it. Somehow, I must find a way to keep on living. Only hoping that somehow, some way, my future would be better, kept me going. Taking a deep breath, I followed the other girls to the bus. I was immune to their cheerful chatter and happy waves of goodbye to the nuns. It would be a long trip home.

CHAPTER SEVENTEEN
GRANDDADDY

I was on the couch, the dull ache in my head refusing to go away. I buried my face in the pillow. I was so tired. Last night, Daddy had rushed Mommy to the hospital again. The doctor said she needed an operation which meant she would be in the hospital a long time.

Grandmother was in the hospital too and also had to have surgery. With both of them in the hospital, I had to drop out of school again. Lifting my head from the pillow, I stared dully out the window. Absently, I scratched painfully at my private area. It was red and inflamed, itching and burning terribly without relief. With a sinking heart, I noted the old, red Chevy crawling along the road. Granddaddy was on his way over.

Things with Granddaddy had started slowly. The worst thing about him was his hard, horny, old hands. He liked to kiss me on the mouth, and he kept trying to make me take my shirt off. I had tried to stay away from him but, now, with Mommy and Grandmother in the hospital, I had no way to escape him.

In my desperation to escape, I had even turned to Daddy for help. I told him that Granddaddy was touching me in private places and kissing me on the mouth. To my surprise he was not surprised or even angry.

"Yeah, Baby, he fooled with your mother when she was little," he had said, his lip curling in contempt. "That's one of the reasons why you can't tell her about us. He really messed her up. Just try to stay away from him." Daddy had offered no help.

Now, I sat up as Granddaddy came through the kitchen door. "Hello, Baby," he said. He cupped his fingers around my chin and aimed a kiss at my mouth. I turned my head, but his lips still grazed mine. At the same time, he ran one hand over my chest and his hard fingers squeezed a nipple. My irritated privates thumped painfully, and I squirmed away from him.

"I hear Marvin crying," I lied and ran into my parent's bedroom where Marvin lay in his crib, fast asleep.

"He's sleeping," Granddaddy followed me into the bedroom. "Why don't you lay on the bed? Take your shirt off. When I'm finished washing the dishes, I'll check your back for pimples."

My heart pounded with fear. "No, sir, I'll wash them," I said. I was afraid of Granddaddy.

"I'll do them, Baby, you just relax." Granddaddy rubbed my back slowly with his hand and handed me an open package of fig cookies. He knew I loved them.

"Yes, sir," I said resignedly. While he was washing dishes, I would have to think of a way to make him leave me alone.

"Come here." Granddaddy pulled me into his arms and, bending his head, kissed me slowly on the mouth. He patted my bottom, and made his way into the kitchen, whistling. As soon as I heard the clink of dishes, I tiptoed to Marvin's crib. Shaking him awake, I scooped him up and propped him on a pillow. Sitting beside him, I kissed his rosy face as he gurgled with pleasure. I sighed with relief. I did not think Granddaddy would bother me in front of the baby.

"Hungry, Dee Dee!" Marvin chortled. He couldn't say Chrissy.

"Okay, Pumpkin," I tweaked his nose. Jumping to my feet, I picked him up. When I brought him into the kitchen, I could see that Granddaddy was disappointed.

"Baby's awake and hungry!" I said, cheerfully.

Granddaddy grunted in reply. He finished the dishes and stomped out the back door. Heart aching, I watched his car as it crunched down the driveway. I could not understand what had happened to my grandfather. I used to love him, and spending time with him was something I had once looked forward to.

Going to spend the day with Grandmother and Granddaddy had been a privilege my brothers, sisters and I had fought over. Granddaddy spent hours telling us long, silly stories. His gray eyes would twinkle behind the black, horned rimmed glasses, and I would study the face, that was so much like Mommy's. He had a strong bone structure, with high cheek bones which proclaimed his Indian heritage. His smile was wide and gentle, and I found his voice deep and soothing. Granddaddy's strong hands made me feel safe. He taught me how to fish and bought me my first fishing pole. He gave up hours of sleep, rising early in the morning to take us fishing. He let me climb on the windmill over the well and taught me not to be afraid of the cows in the pasture.

Grandmother made nap time special. A tiny woman with green eyes, she had great strength of character. She gave us treats of salted peanuts and lemon drops and made us a thick pallet of quilts for sleeping on the living room floor. Grandmother's house was always peaceful, and I loved spending time there. I would listen to the steady hum of the water cooler, as I read my books and lay on the living room floor. Occasionally, I was even allowed to stay overnight.

But things had begun to change last Christmas. We had gone to grandmother and granddaddy's house as usual. I spent time with my cousins, racing about outdoors playing. We ran through the fields looking for milk weed pods to burst open. It was fun to play with the sticky cotton. We stayed away from the barn and teased the cows from a distance. My cousin Elizabeth and I joined hands to play red rover. My eyes looked at the blue, blue, sky and the green trees. I breathed in the scent of rich, pastureland and felt utterly content. I believed there was no place better in the world to be then granddaddy's house at Christmas time.

Later, I had gone into Grandmother's bedroom to look at some of my presents. I had brought my new Barbie doll to play with. Granddaddy had followed me into the bedroom, and I turned to give him a big hug.

"Thank you for the pajamas and the flashlight!" I cried.

"You're welcome, honey," Granddaddy had said as he bent to kiss me, a kiss that made me so uneasy, that I backed away from him, unbidden memories flooding my mind when. I was eight years old and climbing onto the windmill in front of Grandmother's big old white house. I bumped my chest against a beam of wood and was astonished at the sudden pain. I climbed down and ran into the house. Going into the bathroom, I pulled up my shirt and examined my chest. Two swelling knobs had replaced my flat chest. I turned this way and that, examining my changed body in the mirror. Pulling my shirt back into place, I headed for the yard. In the hallway, I bumped into Granddaddy. He pulled me into his arms, kissed me on the mouth, and ran his hand over my breasts. As he held me, clouds of half memories, like birds, beat around my head. I seemed to see Granddaddy bending over me, his face distorted and red. Sharp pains were tearing my body in half. I shook my head and pulled sharply away from Granddaddy. I was confused and stared at my grandfather like I had never seen him before. Granddaddy never said a word just went into the bathroom like nothing had happened.

Now, Granddaddy pulled me into his arms again, rubbing my back in a strange, new way, kissing me with his mouth wide open. He was like the Granddaddy in the hallway, the Granddaddy who had grabbed me, and kissed my mouth when I was eight years old. I did not want this Granddaddy to touch me. I didn't like this Granddaddy. I sensed this Granddaddy wanted me to be close to him. I had run.

Now, with Marvin in my arms, I hugged my baby brother hard. I did not dare think of all the things Daddy, Donald, and Granddaddy wanted me to do. I was so frightened. I was terrified of getting pregnant. I did not know what I would do if I should become pregnant, with my father's, or my brother's, child.

Staring over the top of Marvin's head, I was pensive. I didn't know how long I could hold them all off. I felt that I would go crazy, thinking about it all. Most of the time I couldn't let myself think about it. Someday, something would have to give. I was afraid that it would be me.

Sighing, I once again rubbed frantically at my swollen private area. I wished Mommy were home to give me some soothing medicine to cool the burning itch. Since I had been a small child, I had often become irritated in that region. Sooner or later the burning itch would pass. I hoped my problems would pass away as well.

CHAPTER EIGHTEEN
DESPAIR

Brring! The jangle of the telephone broke the early morning quiet. Hurrying from the bathroom, a can of soap powder in my hands, I ran to answer it. Brring! Breathless, my hands still slippery with cleaning powder and water, I spoke into the receiver. "Hello, Anderson residence!"

"Hi, kid!" It was the bright voice of my best friend.

"Theresa, how neat! What's doing?"

"Aw, nothing. School is boring. I have a cold so Mom let me stay home today. I knew you were home because of your mom. How is she?"

"The same. No better. I guess I'll go back to school someday."

"Yeah, that's rough. Hard to keep up your grades. But all that free time must be groovy."

"No, not really. It gets tiresome. I have lots of work to do around here. There's no one to talk to." Before I knew it, we were launched into conversation. I lay on the kitchen floor, legs crossed in the air, and laughed over the latest gossip with Theresa. Sister Ester had chased one of the eighth-grade boys, hitting him over the head with an umbrella. Shelly was going with Mike, which was a real surprise because he and Judy had been going together since first grade. We were talking about Theresa's day, when our conversation was abruptly interrupted.

"I have an emergency call from Mercy Anderson," the clipped voice of the operator came through the wire.

"Goodbye, kid, hope everything's okay!" Theresa hung up quickly.

Mommy's voice blasted into my ear, "What's the matter with you?"

"What do you mean, Mommy? What's wrong?"

"I've been trying to get you for an hour! This line has been busy for a solid hour!"

"An hour?" I was bewildered. "Theresa just called a few minutes ago, Mommy."

"I said I've been trying to reach you for an hour!"

"Theresa and I were talking. I haven't seen her for a long time."

"Irresponsible!" My mother said bitterly. "You are so irresponsible. I can't count on you. I'm lying here, in this hospital bed trying to get well, and you're on the phone chattering with your friends all the time!"

"No, Mommy, not all the time," I protested.

"Shut up!" Mommy blazed. "I'm talking to you!" This person did not sound like my mother.

"Yes, ma'am," I said.

"Your grandfather says that you never help him with the work. He says all you do is lay around all day, watch T.V. and eat cookies. He is very unhappy with you. If he is good enough, Christian enough, to come and help you with your responsibilities, you should be grateful! Do you understand, Christine?"

"Mommy, I understand, but that just isn't true. I work hard!" I cried.

"Shut up! Your grandfather wouldn't lie! I want you to do whatever he tells you. Is that clear?"

I shut my eyes in despair If Mommy knew some of the things Granddaddy wanted me to do! Despite Daddy's warning not to tell her, I had gone to her several weeks ago.

"Mommy, Granddaddy keeps trying to touch me," I had told her.

Mommy had closed her eyes as if in pain. "He used to touch me too," she had said, in a voice I had to strain to hear. "Try to stay away from him, Christine. Don't be alone with him if you can help it. And please, don't tell Grandmother. It would only worry her."

"Christine!" Mommy's voice blasted in my ear. "Did you hear what I said?"

"Yes, ma'am." I said hopelessly. Could Mommy have forgotten what I had told her? I knew Granddaddy must have complained about me. He was angry because I would not let him touch me.

"Christine, I can't get well if I have to worry about you all the time. Do you think I like being sick? Do you think I like being here?"

"No, ma'am."

"Then do your part! It is your responsibility to look after the little ones. You are to help your father. Obey him, and your grandfather. I don't want Granddaddy to upset your grandmother by complaining about you. At her age, it is very hard to get over surgery. Do you want your grandmother to get well?"

"Yes, ma'am."

"Then act a little more adult!" Mommy slammed the phone down. I sat holding the receiver in my hand. Tears welled in my eyes. It's all too much, I can't take anymore, I can't, I thought drearily, even as my mind was flashing to the night before.

I was lying in the big bed with Daddy. I was naked because he had taken away my clothes. His hands were stroking me. Strange feelings were running through my body. Daddy said softly, "I'm going to take that cherry," and pushed my legs apart and climbed on top of me. I could feel his hard penis slipping inside of me and I pushed at him with my hands.

"Stop, Daddy! Please stop!" I was almost crying in my fear. "I'm afraid of getting pregnant."

Daddy had laughed and rolled off. He cupped my face in one hand and kissed me lingeringly on the mouth, his small green eyes loving. His big belly spilled over to the side while his hands continue to stroke me.

"I got a little, Baby, I sure did! One of these days I'll get the rest. Suck it," he ordered as he pushed my head between his legs and his penis into my mouth.

Dully, my mind returned to the present. Tears splashed on my hands. I'm so dirty, I thought. God, I'm so dirty and impure. If Mommy knew about me and Daddy, she would hate me. When I die, I'll go straight to hell. God won't want me in His heaven.

Maybe, I thought, when you die you don't go anywhere. Maybe what Daddy says is true and there is no God. Maybe if I died, I would have peace. Maybe it would be the end of all this misery. I got up from where I had been lying on the floor. Going into the bathroom, I turned on the water full force. I opened the medicine cabinet. My eyes roamed from the razor blades to the bottle of sleeping pills. I knew about the sleeping pills, and I knew they made you sleep a long time. Mommy used them, and I had even taken the bottle away from her when she had tried to take too many. I knew she had tried to kill herself with them, so they would work for me.

I picked up the bottle of pills and shook several red capsules into my hand. I looked at them; turning them so little lights glinted off their red surface. They were almost pretty, so shining and red in the light. I opened my mouth and brought the handful of pills toward me. As I started to shove them into my mouth, I began to see pictures in my mind. I saw Marvin, his baby face all rosy with love. I saw little Tracey and Anne, left behind for Daddy to abuse. I saw Tommy, his beautiful green eyes filled with tears. I saw Mommy, left alone to cope with Daddy and all the small children. I saw myself in a fiery hell, burning and screaming in eternal torment.

"No!" I screamed and hurled the pills across the bathroom. "I don't want to die!" I ran into the living room and threw myself on the couch, my body shaking with sobs. I couldn't stop crying. I shook with even greater horror, as I contemplated what I had almost done. If I had taken the pills, and failed to die, Daddy would have made me wish I had never been born.

After a long time, my gulping sobs began to ease. Raising my head from the couch, I winced from the awful headache pain. My eyes cleared and I looked out the window toward the road. Inching its way along the drive was Granddaddy's red Chevy. Numb, I watched the car roll to a stop in front of the house. Iron bars seemed to clang around me as I watched Granddaddy slam the door.

They can't destroy me, I thought, and they can't break me. I will be okay. If I can survive today, I can survive anything. They can take my body and do what they want, but they will never destroy me. In my mind rang the single clear thought, I will survive.

CHAPTER NINETEEN
MOVING

I shoved my pigtails away from my sweating face. The tires on the bus hummed with steady monotony. I rested my face against the glass of the partially opened window. This was the third day of the long bus ride to California, where Mommy and Daddy were waiting for us at the bus station in Fremont. After living fourteen years in Texas, Daddy felt he could make more money in a new place. We were moving to a new home.

Daddy had decided to change jobs. His long job search had landed a job as Circulation Director on the Fremont newspaper. Four weeks earlier, he and Mommy had left in the old car, pulling a small trailer behind it. The trailer contained our dishes and clothes, things we would need in our new home. Our little house along with all the furniture was sold, and most of our personal belongings were put into storage.

Mitchell and I remained in Texas with the smaller children. Daddy had rented an apartment in Arlington, and we lived there the month he and Mommy were gone. Since all the beds had been removed, we slept on the floor in a large walk-in closet. The air conditioning was set at a low temperature, and we huddled together at night for warmth. All that long month I cared for Tommy, Tracey, Anne and Marvin. We had to be very careful going in and out, because no adults must know that we had been left alone.

Donald had enlisted in the army shortly before Mommy and Daddy had left for California. That had been a horrible time. Mommy had cried for days without stopping. I could hardly bear to look at her sad face. She wandered through the house, tears streamed down her face, and she refused to smile, no matter how hard I tried to make her happy. Daddy was worried because she was not sleeping at night. He took matters into his own hands and forced her to take several sleeping pills along with a glass of vodka at night so she could sleep. Mommy did not want to drink the vodka. I hid my face in the pillow and covered my ears, so I would not hear Daddy slapping her. Mommy cried piteously for him to stop, but Daddy would not listen. She must drink the vodka and take the pills.

Now, we were finally arriving in California. As the bus ground to a halt, I hoped that those dreadful days were behind us. I fought the dread that tried to overtake me and crowded to the front of the bus. I saw Mommy and Daddy standing to the side of a large group of people. I stepped down and smiled into Mommy's eyes. I thought Daddy would welcome us, but he only hurried us all into the car.

The car moved through the streets and I looked with interest at the houses. California was very different from Texas. We were surrounded by mountains and the houses rolled gently up and down hills. Some of the houses were green or yellow stucco, and the place was filled with fruit trees. How lovely! It was very different from the flat Texas countryside.

We stopped in front of a small white house on a quiet street. Following Mommy and Daddy inside, I was struck by how cool it was. Boxes of dishes were crammed into the small kitchen, and blankets were strewn about the living room floor. All the floors were covered with scratchy, green, indoor-outdoor carpeting. There were sliding glass doors at the rear of the house that opened into a small back yard crowded with lemon and orange trees. Tomatoes grew in a small garden by the fence. A large homemade swing rocked gently from the overhead branches of an ancient tree.

"I've had no time to unpack," Mommy was saying, "we just found this place a couple of days ago."

"Christine can help you unpack," Daddy said.

"Now?" I asked exhausted.

"Yes, you can get started," Daddy said.

I followed Mommy into the crowded white kitchen. An ancient refrigerator growled in the corner. The old-fashioned double sinks were white, chipped enamel. Together, Mommy and I began to unwrap dishes and place them in the cupboards.

"We can wash them later," Mommy said. "Chrissy, I think you kids will like this place. This is a new beginning for us. Daddy likes his new job, and in a couple of weeks school starts."

School! I dreaded the thought. At the age of fourteen I was still in the eighth grade.

"It's so pretty here," Mommy continued. "I am sure we can be happy. If only Donald were here with us! I can't tell you how much I miss him. I feel so guilty, that Daddy forced him into the army at such a young age. I know he would rather be with us."

I didn't answer. If Mommy only knew how relieved I was that Donald wasn't with us. I was glad he was gone. The week before he left, he had pulled me into his closet. Insisting that I remove my pants, he had inserted the head of his penis into my vagina. Even now, I did not understand why I had not fought with him to stop. I stood like a doll and let him do whatever he wanted to. I felt so bad about Donald! I gave him what he wanted because Daddy did not love him. I felt powerless to resist him, and I wanted him to love me. I wished I could understand how I felt about my big brother. Sometimes I hated him; sometimes I was overcome with love for him.

After that incident, I had lived in terror that I might be pregnant. I did not know how to protect myself. Thank God, my period had finally started! It had been two weeks late, and I had really been frightened.

"But maybe he can be with us soon," Mommy was still talking. "It will be so nice when he finally gets to come home."

Later that evening, I was finally able to rest from the three-day trip. There were no beds, so we all slept on the floor. Daddy crumpled newspaper that had been packed around the dishes and made a fire to break the chill. I lay on the floor and watched the flickering blues and greens. I could not help feeling excited. Mommy and Daddy sat by the fireplace sharing a cup of California wine.

"I'm sure we will be happy here, Jimmy," Mommy was saying, "it will be a good life for us. Maybe I can even get a job."

I snuggled sleepily into my blankets, my mind echoing Mommy's optimistic words. We were in a new place, making a new life, and maybe from now on everything would be wonderful. Donald was gone, moved away from home and would spend years in the army. I was finally safe from him. We had moved away from Granddaddy; he could never touch me anymore. Maybe I could even make some friends, who would come over and see what a nice family I had. My mind began to weave a fantasy, complete with parents who loved me, friends, money to spend, and plenty of nice clothes to wear. I would be popular at school, and boys would date me. Mommy and Daddy would let me have lots of free time to be with my friends. I wouldn't have to do housework or keep the younger kids.

My mind went on inventing people to fill my fantasy world. These people would like and admire me. I wouldn't be afraid to try new things, and I would be good at sports. I would be able to sing, dance, and go out for cheer leading.

Best of all, Daddy would treat me like a normal daughter. He would hug me when I did good things and help me with my homework. He would never, ever again touch me in those bad ways. He would be proud of me, and we would forget all the terrible things that had happened in the past.

Becoming drowsy, I let go of my fantasy as it merged into a dream world, where I was running and singing in the California sun. Drifting into sleep, I was sure California would be the answer to all my hopes.

CHAPTER TWENTY
GROWING UP

"This is a wonderful novel! You students will love it." I looked doubtfully at the book Miss Simons pressed into my hand. The assignment was to read the first three chapters before class tomorrow. As the bell rang, I followed the other eighth grade students out into the yard.

I scuffed my shoes through the autumn leaves on the walk home. Frowning at a hole in the toe of one worn tennis shoe, I hitched the books more firmly under my arm. I walked alone, because I had not made friends with any of the other students. I was almost fifteen years old, and still in the eighth grade!

But today I was preoccupied and unconcerned about my lack of friends. I was wrestling with a new feeling. Yesterday, Daddy had introduced me to one of his staff. I had laughed with the young man because his name was Chris, just like mine. He was twenty-two years old and I couldn't stop thinking about him.

He had laughing blue eyes, and when he had taken my hand, he'd given it a little squeeze. He was very, very, nice and I liked him right away. Now as I walked, scuffing the leaves out of my path, I wondered if he had a girlfriend.

Reaching the house, I twisted the knob on the kitchen door. As I pushed it open, I noticed the house was quiet. No cooking smells greeted me, so I knew I had to fix dinner. I investigated the refrigerator. Except for a package of ground beef and a large onion, it was almost bare. Pulling the meat out, I dumped it into a large bowl. Chopping onions and breaking eggs, I began to prepare a large meatloaf. I would bake potatoes to go with it.

Scrubbing potatoes, my thoughts turned to school. I hated it. Almost every day something awful happened. This morning on my way to school a high school boy had walked past me. As we drew even to one another, his hand shot out and grabbed my breast. I was mortified and stunned. I couldn't imagine why he had done that.

At school I had no friends. The kids looked at me funny and made fun of my

Texas accent. When I had pulled my locker open in gym class this morning, a folded bit of paper had fallen out. Curious, I opened it and began to read.

"Dear Stupid," it said, "why are you so queer? Why do you wear the same dress all the time? Why don't you wear socks or stockings? Why do you wear those stupid sandals when it's so cold out?" The note was signed, "Your enemy."

I had stood stock still. The room spun and rocked around me. I was used to kids thinking I was weird. I was used to not having any friends. But this note was hateful. I felt the writer must be staring at me this very minute. Cheeks burning, I had torn the note in little bits and thrown it inside my locker. I looked awkwardly at the holes in my tennis shoes. This pair and my sandals were the only shoes I owned. I didn't have any socks or stockings to wear. I knew all the kids must be laughing at my clothes. I had wanted to run home and hide.

"Chrissy?" Mommy's voice interrupted my thoughts, "is that you?" Mommy stumbled into the kitchen. "Good girl! You started supper." Her voice was funny, and her words were slurred. The sickening smell of stale wine floated around her.

She must be having trouble sleeping, I thought. Lately, Mommy had begun drinking when she couldn't sleep. There was always a bottle of wine or a bottle of vodka sitting in the refrigerator. Now, I rinsed my hands and kissed her cheek. She smiled.

"How was school?" she asked, lighting a cigarette.

"Fine." I reached over and took the cigarette from her fingers. Inhaling deeply, I passed it back to her. Mommy pulled a jug of wine from the refrigerator. Splashing some into a cup, she seated herself at the table.

"Tell me about your day," she invited.

"Nothing special, just the usual," I shrugged. "Mommy, I hate school. I want to drop out."

"Don't do that. Your grandparents took me out of school in the sixth grade to work on the farm. I always regretted it."

"Yes, I know." Inwardly, I sighed. I had heard this sad story many times before.

I quickly changed the subject. "Is Chris coming over tonight?"

"I think so."

"He's pretty nice." I said in an offhand way. Then, changing the subject again I asked, "May I stay home from school tomorrow?"

"No, maybe the day after," Mommy said.

"Okay," I said, "thanks, Mommy."

Later at dinner, I blushed deeply as Chris praised my meatloaf.

"Watch out," he smiled, "someone will marry you in a hurry!"

"Uh-huh!" I said, laughing.

After washing the dishes, I sat on the floor and listened while Daddy played his guitar. Chris sang, and Mommy did, too. I watched every move Chris made. Always smiling, every now and then he would look at me and wink. All too soon it was time to say good night.

Later, I lay on my sleeping bag, by the side of Mommy and Daddy's bed. There still were not enough beds in the house to go around. Daddy said I must sleep by their bed in case Mommy needed me in the night. I tensed myself as I heard Mommy's even breathing.

Although I hoped against hope, the hand groped its way into my sleeping bag and began to fondle me. I lay on Daddy's side of the bed, and it was his hand touching me, as he touched me every night. Even though I feigned sleep, his hand found its way into my pajamas. First, he touched my breasts, teasing the bare nipples under my pajama shirt. His hand then slid into my pajama pants and wiggled into the opening between my legs. In spite of myself, my breathing came faster and faster. Daddy would only stop when he felt I had achieved a climax. Finally, he withdrew his hand and I could go to sleep.

The next morning, I was struggling with a pop quiz on the new novel in English class, when two strange ladies came to the classroom door. Miss Simons greeted them, and they held a whispered conversation.

"Christine," Miss Simons waved at me.

I looked up.

"Please go with these ladies," Miss Simons gestured toward them. The taller lady turned to me with a smile. "I am Mrs. Western," she said, "and this is Mrs. Kelly. We are from the P.T.A."

"Oh," I said, wondering what these ladies wanted with me.

"Your teacher contacted us," Mrs. Western paused and looked uneasy.

"We understand you need some new clothes," Mrs. Kelly jumped in to help her out.

"Oh," I said again. How embarrassing! Two strange ladies were talking to me about my clothes.

"And shoes and stockings," Mrs. Western finished. "We've come to take you shopping."

"Oh," I said a third time.

"We've already contacted your mother, and we're going right now, just as soon as we sign you out."

My embarrassment grew as I followed these ladies down the hall. It continued to grow as I got into their car with them, and, by the time we pulled up in front of the Salvation Army Thrift Store, it almost swallowed me.

With fascination, I watched as the two ladies went through the racks, pulling down dresses they thought would fit me. Although I was grateful for their interest, most of the dresses looked several years old. I stood like a doll in front of the mirror. I was pleased with the attention, and some of the dresses were pretty, but I felt uneasy. I did not think these dresses would fit in with what the other kids wore at school. Finally, the ladies were satisfied with the pile of dresses and we left.

Our next stop was a shoe store where Mrs. Western and Mrs. Kelly allowed me to pick out a pair of shoes. The shoes were brand new, and I picked a sturdy pair of brown and white oxfords. Happily, the ladies dropped me off at home with two large shopping bags filled with clothes. I thanked them as they pulled away. They really had been kind to me. Slowly, I went inside to show Mommy my new clothes.

She thought the clothes were very nice. "Well, I suppose it's nice that the ladies took an interest in you," she said. "I told them so when they called. Now, at least you have something different to wear to school. Did you thank the ladies?"

"Of course!" I replied with dignity.

The next morning, I carefully picked a dress to wear to school. I really didn't want to go, but Mommy said I must.

"You need to be in school." she said firmly.

My steps dragged, as I entered the school yard. My heart beat hard, and I wanted to turn around and run.

Although I had chosen my dress carefully, I had an uneasy feeling that it was all wrong. It was a white dress covered with pretty flowers. The skirt stood out in a wide hoop around my knees. At one time it was meant to be a party dress. I thought it was pretty, but it clashed dramatically with the miniskirts worn by the other girls. As I walked to class, I heard snickers around me.

"How queer!"

"What a square."

"Who dressed her?"

"Hey, where's the hop, Baby?"

"She's way out! Really weird!"

Somehow, I floundered up the steps and into the hall. A cute boy I had thought liked me, snickered as I walked by. I ran pell-mell for the girl's rest room. Once inside, I locked the stall and burst into tears, my sobs muffled by both hands. I stayed in the bathroom until the bell rang. When it was quiet in the hall, I burst from the bathroom and ran and ran. I ran through the gate and all the way down the street to my house, ran inside and slammed the door. The house was quiet.

I went into the bedroom and opened the closet door. Inside, it was dark and cool. I walked into the closet and crouched on the floor. My heart ached with pain. With my arms locked around my knees, I stayed there in the dark listening and thinking. Even after I heard Mommy come home, I crouched on the floor in the dark. I ignored the hunger pains that clawed at my stomach and stayed in the closet until I heard Tommy come home from school. Only then, did I ease the door open and come out. Mommy would think I'd just gotten home. The closet had been a good hiding place something I would remember again when I needed to escape.

CHAPTER TWENTY-ONE
INSANITY

    Walking home from school, my heart was light. My report card was tucked safely in my math book. I couldn't believe I was almost through the eighth grade at last! My grades were good, and I was proud. Maybe I was still not going to school every day, but at least I would pass into high school by the end of the year.

    "Mom?" I called for her as I came through the door. "Mother?" at fifteen, I refused to call her Mommy. "Oh, Mother," I skipped through her bedroom door, "Mother dear, I have a surprise for you!" I saw Mommy lying on the bed, but something about her stopped my laughter. She was strange, changed in some way different.

    "Mommy?" I approached the bed. My questioning turned into fear. "Mommy, what's wrong?" I shouted in terror.

    Mommy looked at me with wild eyes. Her mouth opened and closed. "Da da da, uh da dah!" Gibberish came out of her open mouth. Her fingers flew like birds, like claws, and she plucked at things in the air. She lay on the bed and laughed at me.

    "The bed floats in the air," she giggled. "Tiny squabs fly in the air with me. I catch them like this!" Her fingers clawed the air again. "They are red, red! Red like blood, they are free! I will ride the wind with them!" Mommy's mouth stretched open, and insane laughter ripped the air. Then the laughter turned to moans. "Mo, yo, ooh," she cried. Her eyes rolled upwards, and she was still.

    "Oh, Mommy," I sobbed, "I don't understand! What's wrong with you? Please, please, talk to me!"

    The horrible moaning began again and was followed by the wild laughter. Mommy rose from the bed, and still laughing, she staggered into the hallway. A look of intense concentration crossed her face. Urine splattered down her legs, and onto the carpet. She stooped and paddled her fingers into the puddle.

    "Mommy!" Shocked, I rushed to her, and helped her to her feet. Mommy ignored me and, turning, she walked to a corner of the bedroom. Seating herself on the floor, she pretended to eat, although no food was there.

Wild with terror, I flew to the telephone. "Come home, Daddy," I cried into the receiver, "come home now! Something is terribly wrong with Mommy!"

In ten minutes, Daddy was home and ran into the bedroom. He called Mommy's name, as I followed close behind him.

"Mercy!" his voice was stern as he held her in his arms, "snap out of it! Goddamn it, don't do this!" he slapped her lightly on the face.

Mommy stirred and grinned a horrible clown smile. Her tongue flicked out, and she growled deep in her throat. "I hate you!" she hissed at him. Her head lolled back, and her fingers began to claw the air.

For three horrible days we took care of Mommy at home. On the fourth day, Daddy couldn't deal with her any longer, and said she must go to the hospital. I sat by the telephone while he called for an ambulance.

By then, even I knew Mommy needed to go to the hospital. She kept urinating on herself. That afternoon she had picked up a trash can and thrown it at me in a rage. Another time she had caught me in her arms and covered my mouth with kisses. She seemed to think I was Daddy. As her hands had squeezed my body, I had broken away from her in disgust. Running to the bathroom, I spat out her soft kisses, and washed my face to remove the contact. She disgusted me and I was afraid of her. I had never seen her this way.

The red lights of the ambulance bounced off the white walls of the empty living room. Two men in white coats carried a stretcher into the bedroom. I heard Mommy screaming, "Bitch! Bitch!" The men carried her, strapped on the stretcher, into the living room. Mommy looked at us, her face filled with hate. "Goddamn you all to hell!" she screamed, as the men carried her out the door. I could see her struggling on the stretcher even as she disappeared into the back of the red and white ambulance. The men shut the door, and I watched as the ambulance holding Mommy pulled away.

Daddy turned to me with a terrible look. "All of you go into the bedroom!" he ordered.

The familiar dread clutched at me, replacing the icy despair I had felt for days. I followed Mitchell, Tommy, Tracey, Anne and Marvin into the bedroom. Daddy walked grimly behind us. "Get on your knees!" he ordered. Bewildered, we obeyed.

"All of you stay on your goddamn knees until I say you can get up," Daddy said. "It's your fault she's sick. Every goddamn one of you drove her to it. I don't want to see a smile; I better not hear anyone laugh. I'll make you wish you were dead! Understand? Say your prayers. And you damn well better beg the Blessed Virgin Mary to make her well! Goddamn selfish bunch of kids! I wish you had never been born!"

I wished so too, as I knelt for what seemed like hours. I could see the little ones swaying on their knees. Anne and Tracey began to cry. Marvin lay on the floor and his little eyes closed in sleep. I looked at Mitchell, and I knew he could not help them. It was up to me to talk to Daddy. Timidly, I crept into the living room where Daddy sat in the dark.

"Please, Daddy," I begged, "can't the little ones go to bed? They're so tired."

Daddy roused himself with a start. "Go to bed, every goddamn one of you!" he bellowed. Go ahead! Sleep while they put your mother in a loony bin! Selfish, goddamn brats!"

I ran into the bedroom. "Go to bed, now! Don't say a word," I instructed in a whisper, "go on before he changes his mind." In a minute, the bedroom was empty. I didn't hear a sound as the little ones got into bed. I tucked Marvin in and went back into the living room where Daddy still sat in the dark.

"Come here," I went to the chair where he sat. Daddy pulled me into his arms. I could tell he wanted to talk. "Tomorrow, you will go with me to see your mother," he said.

The next day I went with Daddy to the hospital. Mommy was in a large room with several other people. The walls and floor were covered with thick, white padding. An iron door with a small window made of thick glass closed Mommy in. I felt horror, and other feelings I could not name, as I looked through the small window and into the room.

I could see Mommy sitting in a corner on the floor. She was eating where there was again no food. Looking up, she caught sight of Daddy. She ran to the door and her lips stretched wide in a smile of pleasure.

The guard unlocked the small door. Ignoring me, Mommy burst through the door and jumped into Daddy's arms. Her long brown hair was held back by a wide headband, and she looked about seventeen years old. Her blue eyes shone with pleasure.

"Jimmy, darling! How I've missed you!" she cried. She kissed Daddy passionately. "I was hoping you would see me tonight!" She turned to the guard holding a cigarette in her hand. "Light my cigarette," she instructed.

The whole time we were visiting, Mommy acted like I wasn't there. She sat with Daddy in the visitor's lounge and cuddled in his lap. She stroked his hair and kissed him on the mouth. Finally, the nurse said it was time to leave. Mommy did not tell me goodbye.

Together, Daddy and I left Mommy in that awful place. She waved goodbye, blowing kisses to Daddy, and promising to see him soon.

Back at home, I ran to check on the little ones. Mitchell had put them to bed, and they were sleeping. Mitchell was sleeping too. I went into the kitchen and Daddy took me into his arms.

"You'll have to drop out of school," he said. "I need you to hold this family together. You must be mother to us all." A funny look crossed his face. "Your mother's damn selfish!" he said.

I looked at Daddy in surprise. "She can't help it," I said. Pulling away from him, I leaned against the refrigerator. Tears ran down my face. Gulping sobs, I couldn't control shook my body. I buried my face in my hands and cried. All the horror of the past few days rose up inside me. I couldn't stop crying.

Daddy grabbed my hands and pulled them away from my face. "Don't fall apart on me! You're the only one strong enough to hold this family together. You keep us all going, baby." He caressed my face with his hand, "I need you so, baby. God, I need you."

He gently led me into the living room and urged me to sit on the floor. Going into the kitchen, he returned with two glasses full of wine. Handing me one, he seated himself beside me. I only sipped at my wine, not liking the taste. Daddy lit a cigarette and handed it to me.

"The doctor says your mother will probably never get any better. She may be this way the rest of her life. I think we better try to get used to the idea."

Iron bars seemed to clang around me. Through their shadow, I stared briefly at a future too terrible to contemplate. It would be better for Mommy to be dead, than to spend the rest of her life in that place. "I can't accept it! What kind of a God would do this to her?" I cried out in my anger.

"There is no God," Daddy said.

I didn't answer. I refused to believe there was no God. There had to be a God! Someday he must rescue me from this hell in which I lived. Daddy pulled me to him, his fingers fumbling with my shirt.

I didn't pull away. Deep inside I was still terrified of him. I also loved him and wanted to help him. I let him do as he wanted. I lay there, willing my mind to go blank. I would not feel the prison that held me.

CHAPTER TWENTY-TWO
A MILESTONE

The heavy double doors closed behind me. Exactly one month before my nineteenth birthday, I achieved my ultimate goal. I graduated from high school. True, there was no cap and gown, no graduation ceremony, no prom, but I had something of far greater worth. I had my high school diploma.

I stared reflectively at the grove of trees across the snow-packed road. My warm breath frosted the air. So much had happened since we had moved to Auburn, New York; I felt I needed to catch my breath.

The nightmare in California had faded only slightly in my mind. I still shuddered to remember the first days after Mommy had come home from the hospital. There were the days she stumbled about the house, stoned on sleeping pills and vodka. There were the black days when she did not recognize Daddy or me.

Then, there were days of black fear in Walla Walla, Washington, where we had lived briefly. For two terrible months I had thought I might be pregnant. Those months in Walla Walla were a time of great struggle for me. I became deeply depressed, not caring what I did each day. When Daddy was offered the opportunity to move to Auburn, New York, it seemed like a God sent opportunity. New York had proven to be better than any other place we had lived. Our two-story house, on Perrine St., felt like a real home.

I remembered the grim determination that had brought me to this school. Daddy had told me that going to high school would be my own decision. Marshaling my courage, I had walked with Tommy to school on a balmy day, gone to see the counselor and explained that, I was a unique student. She had listened thoughtfully, and then pulled a form from her bulging desk. Together, she and I had mapped out a program that allowed me to graduate in two and a half years.

So, I had hurried through high school. I never went to a dance, or a football game, and made few friends. Daddy did not allow me to date. I worked in the summertime and after school, at the newspaper and contributed to the needs of the household, paying board of one hundred dollars per month. I was sixteen years old, and I was working and paying rent.

    I made one close friend in school. Her name was Linda, and she helped me, to understand what it was like to have fun. Sometimes, I was allowed to spend the night with her. It was wonderful! We would slip out of her house at night and ride motorcycles with some guys she knew. Together, she and I walked all over Auburn sharing secrets and meeting boys. Linda had a tough home life too. She took care of her younger sisters all the time, so we had a lot in common. Linda became Mitchell's girlfriend, spending time with him during the summers, when he was home from college.

    Through Linda I met Gary. I closed my eyes, reliving the first time I had ever seen him. I had rushed home to tell Mommy all about him.

    "I met a boy!" I told her, bursting through the door.

    Mommy looked up with an indulgent smile. "Tell me about him," she said.

    "He's a friend of Linda's. He has blue eyes and is so cute! He likes me, Mom!"

    The wonder was that he really did like me. I liked him too. I loved his blue eyes and wide-open smile. He was a high school dropout, which bothered me a little, but not enough to keep me from dating him. I began to slip out with him when Daddy thought I was with Linda. Eventually, though, Daddy found out about Gary. Daddy didn't like him one bit. I felt rebellion building within me. I had to find a way to make Daddy leave me alone so I could live my own life.

    I left the school grounds and boarded the bus home. Staring at my snow-crusted boots, I thought about Daddy. He still visited my bed at night. Mommy was working nights as a nurses' aide, and the nightly sex sessions continued, when Daddy would pull me from my bed after my sisters were asleep.

    I wanted out. I was more than ready to leave home.

    Aside from working and paying board, I still had all my former responsibilities. I would run home from school and start cooking dinner. I would then drag out the vacuum cleaner and vacuum, dust, clean the bathroom, and do whatever else needed to be done. After all this, I would rush off to work. Between answering the telephone, and my customer service duties at the newspaper, I would do my homework. Only then would I drag myself home, to a stale dinner and tumble into bed. My days began at sunrise with breakfast to make and lunches to prepare. I worked all day every Saturday. I was beginning to bitterly resent it all.

Even though I was eighteen years old, I couldn't seem to break away from home. School had held me there, but now that I had finished school, the sky was the limit. I could leave home. My life was ahead of me, and Gary could show me how to have fun.

I was almost home. Walking toward home from the bus stop, my feet felt cold and numb. Warmth and comfort were at hand, and soon escape would be at hand, too. Soon, I would be free!

CHAPTER TWENTY-THREE
REBELLION

"But I really want to go to nursing school!" I tried to convince Daddy this was not a passing whim.

"It's funny that you didn't want to go until I decided to go," Mommy said.

It was true that I had never given Mommy and Daddy any reason to think I wanted to be a nurse. I hadn't really thought of it until Mommy began to work as a nurses' aide. The stories she told me about her work had begun to capture my interest. When she had decided to take the exam to qualify for practical nursing school, I had decided to take it too. Mommy and I had both passed although she'd scored higher than I did. Now, Daddy was telling me there was not enough money for me to go.

"You can go later, Christine," Daddy said, "maybe next semester. Now is your mother's time. After all, you have your whole life ahead of you."

Anger churned inside of me. It just wasn't fair! All Mommy and Daddy did was take and take from me. I couldn't even save the money I needed, because I had to give them one hundred dollars every month! Daddy had even borrowed the four hundred dollars I had saved over the summer. I had counted on that money for nursing school. I turned and walked away in disgust.

"Christine! I'm talking to you," my father warned as I walked away. "You're still not too big for me to beat your ass!"

I jerked around, "No, I'm not too big!" I flared back. "You can threaten me, just the way you've always threatened me."

"What are you saying?" Daddy's face was dangerous.

"I'm saying I'm afraid of you! I've always been afraid of you! That's the only reason I ever did anything for you, out of fear!" I knew this was a dangerous truth I was telling him. "But I'm not going to be ruled by you anymore. I can walk out of here anytime I want. I'm over eighteen years old!" I was shaking but defiant in my rebellion.

Daddy grabbed my arm. "So, Miss Smart-Ass! You think you can do whatever you goddamn please! You're over eighteen years old, huh!" Daddy snarled, shaking me until my head snapped back and forth. "I'll go to a judge and have you declared mentally incompetent! I'll get custody of you until you're twenty-five! How would you like that, Smart-Ass?"

"You can't do that!" I backed away in fear.

"Try me," Daddy's eyes were small and mean.

"Chrissy, Daddy, don't," Mommy wrung her hands. "Daddy, you're making her cry."

"I hope she cries her goddamn eyes out," Daddy said.

"I'm leaving," I said quietly. Tears were running down my face. "I can't take it here, anymore."

"Where are you going," Daddy sneered, "to that boyfriend of yours? That dope-head I don't want you seeing?"

"You don't want me seeing anyone!" I shouted, "At least he loves me!"

Daddy jerked me around to face him. "How much does he love you?" he screamed. "How much?"

I looked Daddy in the eye and smiled slowly through my tears. "He loves me enough," I said softly.

Daddy slammed me against the wall. "You bitch," he said slowly and viciously, "I ought to kill you! Get the hell out of my sight!"

Mommy followed me to my room, her eyes brimming with tears. "Where will you go?"

I turned to hug her, "I'll go to my friend Becky."

"Will you come home when he cools off?" Mommy's voice trembled.

I shook my head sadly, "I honestly don't know, Mom."

"Wait," Mommy put her hand on my arm. "Did you mean what you said about Gary?"

I decided not to lie. "Yes, Mom, I did. Gary and I have been sexually close. I went to family planning and got pills after my birthday."

"I can't believe it," Mommy slowly dropped my arm. "I was a virgin until my wedding day. I thought we taught you better than that."

I choked off a bitter laugh. If only Mommy knew how hard I had fought to stay a virgin!

Becky was happy to see me. Her parents were out of town and she was having a wonderful time. I sat sipping a cup of coffee as I told her bits of the scene I had with Daddy.

"That was a bad scene," Becky said in sympathy. "Have you called Gary?"

"As a matter of fact," I said with a nervous laugh, "he's on his way over with Randy!"

"Oh, I'm always glad to see Randy!" Becky smiled. She and Gary's cousin Randy had a thing going.

Half an hour later we sat on Becky's couch passing a joint between the four of us. As they passed me the roach, I held the clips and toked on it hard, a mellow head settling over me. I turned my head and looked into Gary's blue eyes. I quivered at the thrill that passed over me. I loved him so much. I smiled remembering how square I once was, a time when I wouldn't touch grass. I smiled again, remembering the day Gary had told me he used drugs.

"You do what!" I was horrified that Gary smoked pot. We were standing outside his mother's apartment.

"I said I smoke pot. What's wrong with that?"

"It isn't good for you," I said.

"If it bothers you, I'll quit." he took my hand gently. "I would do anything for you."

"Even go back to school?" I pressed him.

Gary threw back his head and laughed, "Even go back to school, little girl."

I smoothed his hair. "Thank you," I said primly.

I had changed my mind about grass one day when we were with his brother. Robert looked like a slightly older version of Gary. We were sitting at Gary's sister's house, and a joint was making the rounds. I sipped a rum and coke and watched them pass the joint around. They seemed to be having such a good time. I leaned over and whispered to Gary.

"You sure?" he asked me.

"I'm sure," I said, "I want to try it, Gary. After all, you seem to enjoy it!"

They passed me the joint, and I toked on it so hard that I coughed. The smoke seared my throat. I tried again. At first, I didn't feel anything, and then a strange feeling took charge of my body. I felt alien, like someone else was in my skin. I panicked and "freaked" out. Gary had sat with me for two hours while I had come down from my high.

"I never saw grass make anyone act like that!" Robert had said, as I alternately laughed and cried.

Returning to the present, I floated in my high. Grass no longer "freaked" me out. I dug into the cookies and chips Becky provided for the munchies. The scene with Daddy seemed unreal, like it had happened to someone else. I did not even feel a part of it.

Later, I lay in the bunk bed above Becky's, and listened to her even breathing. I thought of Gary and his long goodnight kiss. He had wanted to spend the night, but I hadn't wanted to upset his mother. She liked me and I didn't want that to change.

I felt blue and lonesome as I turned over to sleep. I couldn't pretend my daddy hadn't hurt me. Tears trickled down my cheeks as I thought about Mommy. Burying my face in the pillow and cried. Maybe tomorrow would bring the end to my problems.

CHAPTER TWENTY-FOUR

ESCAPE

The hands moved over me. I struggled and whimpered. Cruel and hard, the hands tightened their hold. A mouth was whispering, the hissing voice forming words of longing, of lust. I struggled to escape but could not break the grip of the hands that pinned me to the bed. A wet sucking mouth found my lips and closed tightly. I could not breathe. Suddenly, the mouth lifted, and sweet air rushed into my lungs even as the hissing voice found my helpless ears.

"Pussy," the voice breathed, "sweet pussy! I'm going to get that cherry! All mine; I'll never share you with anyone!"

I struggled to speak. I tried desperately to form words. My mouth, my voice refused to obey. My tongue felt like leather and my vocal cords were frozen.

"No!" Screaming, gasping, the words burst from my throat. "No! No! No!" I pushed the hands aside and sat up in bed. My scream hung suspended in the night. I lay back gasping, my heart pounding as sweat poured from my face. I had been dreaming. The even sounds of night, the ticking clock, and my sister's quiet breathing, brought the room slowly into focus. I was in my own bedroom at home.

I sat on the side of the bed and swung my feet to the floor. My scream had not disturbed the house. I looked at the clock. It was 2:00 a.m. It was strange to be at home, but Mommy's pleas had convinced me. She needed me. An uneasy peace existed between Daddy and me. I sat on the side of the bed and wondered what had brought on the dream about Daddy. Since I had told him about Gary, he had not attempted to touch me.

A floorboard creaked. I stiffened and my hair stood on end. Convinced that my sisters and I were not alone, I looked around fearfully, feeling an unseen presence in the room. Looking at my sleeping sisters, I felt comfort in their company. I was sleeping in their bedroom because I was afraid to sleep alone. Mommy had offered me Mitchell's now empty bedroom, but I didn't want it. I once had a frightening experience in that room. Sleeping soundly one night I was awakened by a blow on the head. I had sat up abruptly. I was alone, yet my head smarted as from a sharp slap. The night had quivered with an evil presence, making it impossible for me to sleep anymore.

Now, I shivered. I remembered afternoons crouched over a Ouija board with Mitchell and Donald, communicating with a "spirit". It talked to us many times, spelling out messages. It told us that it (the spirit) was the ghost of an evil murderer now long dead. Some of the things it told us were truly horrible, prophecies of doom and death and messages of evil things to come.

Uneasy, I listened again, but I heard no more strange noises. Crossing myself, I prayed aloud, "Hail Mary full of grace, the Lord is with thee, please Mother Mary, protect me from evil, now!" Listening to the silence I felt better, and slowly the fear left. I often prayed to Mary when I was afraid.

I lay back down but I wasn't sleepy, and my mind was racing. In two days, I was getting married. As fantastic as it seemed, it was true. Gary and I were getting married.

Much to my surprise, it was Daddy who had suggested the marriage. Gary and I had planned on waiting a few years to give ourselves a chance to become financially secure. After my return home, I had sat with Daddy in his office at the newspaper, making small talk.

"You might as well get married," Daddy said.

Surprised, I looked up from picking at my sweater. My eyes took in the furnishings of the office in a single glance: the shabby desk, file cabinets, and my picture smiling at me from his desktop.

"We plan to eventually," I said carefully.

"Why wait?" Daddy asked, "you didn't wait on anything else."

I blushed.

"Well, all it takes is a good three inches to satisfy you," Daddy sneered, "his thing must be good and hard."

"I don't want to talk about this," I said quietly.

Daddy's demeanor changed and he smiled agreeably, "Why don't you get married?" he pursued. "You are old enough to be on your own. Your mother and I won't stand in your way."

"We might," I said thoughtfully.

Gary and I decided not to wait since the thought of leaving home appealed to me. I was ready to escape the responsibility that had shackled me all my life. At first Gary's mother fought the idea, but he firmly persuaded her that our minds were made up. We began making wedding plans. I pretended not to notice that my own mother was less than joyful. Gary's mother noticed and remarked upon it.

"You mother acts like she doesn't want this wedding," she said, "doesn't she like Gary?"

"Well, of course," I defended Mommy, "she just doesn't have much time. She's in nursing school, you know."

"But you're her daughter! You're going to be married! It seems a little strange that she's so, well, stand-offish. I can't even get her to discuss the wedding."

"She will." I promised earnestly.

At home, I demanded that Mommy meet with Gary's mother.

"She thinks you don't love me," I told her.

"That's ridiculous! I'm just busy with nursing school," Mommy said.

"Mom, you've got to make time. After all, I'm getting married," I told her firmly.

Mommy finally did meet with Gary's mother. I could tell that Gary's family thought mine was a little strange. I didn't worry about it because my family felt the same way about his.

"We don't need our folks," I told Gary.

Now, I was only two days away from the wedding. A glance at the clock told me it was time for sleep. I lay back with anticipation, strange noises in the night forgotten. Gary and I would soon be moving into our own little house. Finally, my life would be wonderful. Marriage would be the answer to all my unhappy years. Everything I wanted was within my reach. All I had to do was grab at life and hold on tight!

CHAPTER TWENTY-FIVE
REALITY

Hunched into my thin coat, I fought the stinging wind. Snow clung to my boots as I crunched through the thin, powdery stuff. My teeth chattered. Low sullen clouds indicated the probability of a long snowstorm. I was cold, tired, and depressed, just like the winter sky. Gary's old ford had broken down again, and I was making the long walk home. Reaching our front door, I turned the knob and went inside. The cold empty house held no welcome for me.

I clumped into the hallway shaking the snow from my boots. Fumbling with the thermostat, I turned the gas heat on high and warm air began to seep through the house. Once my shivering had stopped, I peeled off my boots, and then my coat. I knew from the empty house that Gary must be at his mother's house. That was fine with me because I needed to think. I set the kettle on the stove and measured instant coffee. Seating myself at the rickety kitchen table, I lit a cigarette and propped my tired feet on a chair. Working as a nurses' aide at the convalescent hospital was not all that fun. On top of that, my marriage was not what I had expected.

Our wedding had been small, but beautiful. I was married in my floor length blue velvet dinner dress, and a matching blue veil. It was an intimate ceremony with only family and a few friends present. We then spent two days in a rented room having our 'honeymoon'. I didn't mind the lack of luxury, because I knew we didn't have much money. Basically, Gary and I paid for our own wedding with no help from our parents. I was used to doing without money and I really didn't mind.

The bubbling kettle distracted me. I poured boiling water and brought the coffee to the table. Stirring it, I thought about Gary. Gary had not worked since we had gotten married and we were barely scraping by. Every month, we were short on the rent and we couldn't afford a telephone. Utilities were high and we lived on peanut butter sandwiches and macaroni. My paycheck just did not stretch from pay day to pay day.

Add the price of grass, and a bottle of vodka now and then, there just was not enough money. Gary was going to have to get a job.

There were other things that were bothering me. Gary was wishy-washy. He couldn't seem to say no to people. The tenderness I had found so appealing before we were married seemed to me possessive and clinging now. And there was another problem. I found sexual intercourse almost too painful to endure. Gary didn't know it, but I was beginning to dread our nightly encounters. I felt old at the age of nineteen.

The door banged. "Hi, Chrissy," Gary planted a kiss on my lips, "tired?"

"Uh huh!" I said emphatically. "Those patients seem to get heavier every day."

"So, why don't you get a transfer? You could move to an easier floor."

"No," I said. "I like the second floor even if they are total care patients. Did you get the car fixed?"

Gary shifted. "No, actually I didn't. I was over at Mom's today."

"Gary!" I exploded. "Don't you think I get tired of walking back and forth every day?"

"Hey, there's no problem. Robert promised to lend me his car in the morning."

"We can't depend on Robert and Marla all the time! People get tired of doing us favors! Your sister already calls us free loaders!"

"Well, not Robert he's my brother!" Gary shouted.

"Listen, Gary," I yelled back, "I'm tired of all this responsibility. You've got to get a job!"

Gary's face turned white; his jaw set in anger. "What do you think I've been trying to do? I don't sit around on my ass all day!"

"Ever since my father fired you, you've been out of work," I retorted. "Maybe you should spend less time with your mother and more time looking for work!"

"For your information, Mom agrees with you. She told me to get a job today!" Gary turned on his heel, grabbed his coat, and slammed out the door.

I sighed. From experience, I knew he would be back, full of apologies. This was not the first time we had an argument about work. I felt that something was missing in

Gary. He seemed to have no desire to achieve. I recalled how he had failed the GED exams for his high school diploma. No amount of begging on my part could get him to try again. He seemed contented just the way he was.

Depression hit me. Why can't things be the way I want them to be, I wondered. I had been so sure that marriage would be the answer to my problems. I had been so sure that my life would finally become what I wanted it to be. Tears filled my eyes and I ran to the bedroom. Throwing myself into the rumpled sheets, I pounded my fists against the pillow. Life was so unfair! All I ever wanted was to be happy. I was so tired of being used. I just wanted someone to love me, just the way I had always wanted my parents to love me. Thinking of my parents, I whimpered. Since I had married, they were farther away from me, then ever before.

For the first months of my marriage, I had tried hard to be close to Mommy and Daddy. Now that I was married, I was sure we could be the family I had always wanted us to be. I saw myself having breakfast with Mommy while the two of us discussed husbands. Gary and Daddy would be very close. They might go fishing, or to a ball game. I chose to overlook that Daddy had never even taken his own sons to a ball game. I saw us going on family outings to the park, and I was sure Daddy and I would have a normal father/daughter relationship. Mommy and I would get together and gossip. Eventually, both my parents would proudly look forward to becoming grandparents.

I thought I would continue in my familiar family role of "holding the family together." Daddy would continue to confide in me, and Mommy would need me to be close by. Sadly, things did not work out that way. Whenever I visited Mommy and Daddy, they seemed withdrawn and cold. They were not interested in visiting us. Daddy was barely polite to Gary. Whenever I dropped by on a visit, they were busy with other things. Gradually, I withdrew. I became close to Robert and Marla, Gary's older brother and his girlfriend.

"You guys are my family," I told them over and over, usually, when we were stoned on pot.

The door banged again. Gary was back. Gingerly, he poked his head around the bedroom door.

"I'm sorry, baby," he said. He tiptoed to the edge of the bed and took my hand. "Please don't be sad," he begged, dropping to the floor and burying his face in my lap.

Still troubled, I began stroking his hair. Gary was all I had, but I couldn't pretend that everything was okay. I knew there were problems in our marriage. I wished I knew how to make them go away. Somehow, we would have to work them out. I hoped we could.

CHAPTER TWENTY-SIX
THE TRIP

I sat as the room revolved slowly around me. I watched black, musical notes float from the stereo. Acid rock, the perfect company for acid tripping, blared loud and then soft. I didn't know if the music was so loud it seemed soft, or if it was so soft it seemed loud. Movie pictures flickered against the wall. I watched as the black stereo notes dropped from the sky. They grew legs and began to crawl around the floor. I giggled because they were so fat. Fat, black crawling notes. One tried to squeeze under the door. The walls wavered and dissolved. Cold air rushed into the room. I shivered and turned to Gary at my side.

"Do you feel that wind?" I shouted.

He nodded. "Feels like snow," he screamed above the rushing wind. Suddenly, he was lost in a blinding, white, winter blizzard. I looked around for my coat. My teeth began to chatter. I must find my coat, or I would freeze. The wind began to sob and moan. It beat at me, tearing at my hair, driving snow into my eyes. I cried because I was so cold.

All at once, the raging blizzard stopped. Once again, I sat in my comfortable chair. A fire crackled and blazed in front of me. I was comforted by its warmth and held out my hands. Long burning fingers reached forward to draw me into the fire, to draw me into hell. I huddled in my chair. Covering my face with my hands, I screamed and screamed as crackling laughter and demon whispers snaked through the room.

Gary was standing over me. I felt his arms go around me. I heard the demon laugh and laugh. I looked at Robert, Gary's brother, and his face changed, and horns grew from his head. His eyes shrunk, small and red. I knew he was evil. I screamed and screamed.

"Her trip is bad," I heard Gary say.

Marla took my face into her hand, "Come back, Chris," she called, "come back to us. See, we're all tripping together."

I looked at Marla. No horns grew from her head. I looked at the fire. It was gone. Gary was standing beside me and Robert was sitting on the couch. There were no demons. Had I imagined it all? Had I really screamed? I had no way of knowing.

"Let's go outside," Robert said.

We went out to the snow-covered yard. I was wearing my coat, so I didn't shiver. I watched huge tanks driving down the moonlit street, with German Nazi soldiers sitting in the tanks. Their eyes glinted evil death. I waited for gunfire to fill the streets and kept thinking we should go hide in a ditch so the soldiers wouldn't see us. Robert, Gary and Marla paid no attention to the tanks. I decided not to worry about them.

We were in the car. Bonnie, Gary's older sister, was driving. I knew we were safe because she didn't trip. I wondered where we were going. I looked at the roof of the car. It dissolved and I was staring at swaying black trees. Then, helicopters descended from the sky and hovered over the trees.

"Stop the car, Bonnie," Robert said.

"Are you crazy, Robert? There's nothing out there but frozen water!" Bonnie exclaimed.

"No, Bonnie, it's cool. Stop!"

"Okay, but I don't know what you think you're doing."

We struggled out of the car. As far as the eye could see there was nothing but frozen water. We began running. We were laughing and sliding on the frozen lake in our shoes. Someone had made a bonfire. It crackled and flowed in the lake of ice. I skated through the fire in my shoes.

"Come on! Are you crazy?" I heard Bonnie screaming. "That ice is weak! There must be twenty feet of water underneath! Come on! Get into the car!"

We went back to the car. The tires crunched in the snow as I lay dreamily in Gary's lap. His face was tender, and kind and his eyes were very, very blue. I began to kiss him.

"Hey, you two," Robert called from the front seat, "Cut it out!"

I sat up. We were back at Robert and Marla's apartment. As we got out of the car, I noticed the sky was turning pink. It was nearly dawn.

Once inside, I went to the bathroom. Closing the door, I stared at my mirrored reflection. I was beginning to come down. A spasm of pain shook me. I disliked this part of the trip, the part of coming down, the coming home. Gary, Marla, Robert and I had been together all night. One of the rules of tripping was that you tripped with partners. Since Robert and Marla had turned me on to LSD, we all tripped together almost every weekend. Now I wondered how Bonnie had gotten in on the trip. Maybe I had only imagined her.

Fatigue closed over me. I rinsed my mouth and went to find Gary. "Let's go to bed," I whispered.

"We're gonna crash," Gary told Robert.

"Yeah, man, we're coming down too," Robert said.

Gary and I went to bed. I lay there waiting to come down enough to sleep. Tripping was great, but it took a full twelve hours to do it right. As I began to calm down, I smiled, remembering how square I had once been. Turning over, I listened to Gary's quiet breathing.

Sinking into sleep, the bed felt good. When we got up, we would smoke a few joints. That would put a nice mellow head on the weekend. Monday was far, far away. As long as there was acid, I had no problems. Life was very, very, groovy. I slept.

CHAPTER TWENTY-SEVEN
THE ARMY

"Man, it's the greatest! I mean, it's the greatest! I feel better than I ever did in my whole life. I'm a man, Gary! You ought to try it."

Gary and I looked at each other. An idea glimmered in the back of my mind. I flipped my long, straight hair back over one shoulder as I continued to listen to Gary's cousin Randy talking with enthusiasm.

"At first, I hated it. Basic was the worse, man. But once I got through basic, man, it was great! I mean, you get your choice of duty station, and you come and go as you please. Who knows? I might stay in and see the world!"

"But the army, Randy?" I questioned. "To tell you the truth, I never thought you'd make it. At the very least, I thought you'd hate it."

"I did at first. It was hell. But if you can take basic training, you can take anything."

"I wonder what it's like for women," I mused.

"I don't know, but it would be a great life for Gary. You should try it, man."

"Oh no, you're not getting me into that!" Gary protested.

"Gary," I said, "you ought to think about it. At least find out what it's all about."

"Sure," Randy said, "what can it hurt?"

The next morning Gary and I stood outside the recruiter's office.

"Come in," the sergeant invited, "may I help you?"

"We just wanted some information," I said.

"Well, great! That's what I'm here for," the stocky man smiled. "I'm Sergeant Bill Daniels."

As Sgt. Bill gave Gary the sample test, I studied the pictures on his wall. To my surprise, there were pictures of women in uniform included among those of the men.

"Now, how about you?" Sgt. Bill asked, turning to me. "Are you interest in enlisting?"

"Me?" I asked, surprised.

"Sure. There are lots of opportunities for women in the service these days. The army will train you for a good job."

"I never thought about it," I admitted.

"You should. You're a bright young woman. Could have a good future ahead of you. The army's a good starting place. They will even pay you later to go to college, and you can purchase a home or business on the GI Bill. Lots of great benefits too."

I was sold. "I'm going in, too," I told Gary.

"Great!" he beamed.

One week later, we boarded the bus for the army testing center in Syracuse. I saw only one other woman in the crowd. We arrived at a big building and were seated in an airy classroom. The testing began. We took tests until noon and then broke for lunch. Afterwards, we were examined by a doctor. That night, we slept in an expensive hotel. I enjoyed the whole experience.

The next morning there were more tests. By lunch time, Gary and I were informed we had been accepted as candidates in the army. We were sworn in and given our induction dates.

"I can't believe it all happened so fast," I told Gary on the bus ride home.

"Wait till I tell Mom!" Gary said.

We went together to tell Gary's mother the news.

"I'll miss you," she said, "but I can't help but feel it is a good thing for you to do."

I agreed with her. I was tired of earning the living. It was getting harder and harder for me to go to work. Like demons rearing their ugly heads, my old fears of people were coming back. I woke in cold sweats in the middle of the night. At the end of a day off from work, I would cry uncontrollably just thinking about the next workday. I would try to get sick, so I would have an excuse to call in. How I hated my job! I felt the nurses looked down on me. They thought I was inferior because I was just a nurses' aide. I felt they all talked about me, and I was also tired of my small salary. I needed an escape. The army seemed a good way to make my life better.

"When do you go in?" Mom asked Gary.

"Oh, in June," he said, "a long way off yet."

"At last you'll be working," Mom remarked.

"Oh, yes, he will!" I agreed sweetly. We all laughed.

My parents took the news without much show of emotion. "The army?" Mommy questioned, "Well, I suppose it's a good idea. Maybe you can get some medical training."

"It's probably a good plan," Daddy agreed. He proceeded to boast about his own army days. I could see that he approved.

"Man, you're crazy!" Robert said in horror when we told him. "You're stone nuts! What are you going to do in the army, Gary? Did Chris talk you into this?"

"No," I said indignantly, "it was Gary's own idea."

"Well, it stinks. It'll never work. What do you want to go so far away for, Gary? Your family's here."

"Hey, we have to live," I said getting angry myself, "and Gary needs to work."

"When are you going in?" Robert asked, still angry.

"In June," Gary said. "Don't be mad, man. Please?"

"Okay, man," Robert shook his head, "we'll have a tripping party before you go." He turned to Marla, "Who are we going to party with now?"

Marla just shrugged.

As it turned out, Gary and I decided not to wait until June to leave. I woke up one morning determined not to go back to work.

"I need a vacation," I told Gary. "I can't stand that place any more!"

"You don't have to go back," Gary agreed, "but what are we going to live on?"

"We'll go see Sgt. Bill," I said.

In December of 1974, I waved goodbye to Gary as he boarded the plane to take him to Fort Knox, Kentucky. Turning away from the big glass window with a peculiar, empty feeling, I followed Robert and Marla to their car. I was going to live with them until I left for basic training myself.

    For the first time in my life, I would be without the company of parent or husband. Already, I was missing Gary. Since our marriage, we had been together constantly, yet in a way, I was glad for the separation. No more painful nightly sex sessions. I would be able to close my eyes and just go to sleep. There would be no more noisy arguments over money or work. As the car left the airport, I watched Gary's plane lift into the clouds. For better or worse, our lives had taken a drastic turn.
I wondered what the future would hold next.

CHAPTER TWENTY- EIGHT
CHEATING

I hurried through the darkness. Ahead of me, Janet's figure disappeared in the fog and I had no desire to be lost on this strange base. I broke into a run, and huffing, I caught up with Janet.

"You left me," I said accusingly.

Janet pushed her glasses up her skinny nose. "I didn't mean to," she said, "I guess I'm just excited."

"What do you think it will be like?" I asked. The smell of Magnolia blossoms hung heavy in the air. The night was thick and humid.

"I loved basic training," Janet said. "I hope it will be just as nice here."

I didn't bother to answer. The fact that she had loved basic training was amazing. I was just thankful that basic was over. For me, it had been a horrible experience. I hoped I would never smell pine oil or shoe polish again. As we hurried toward the dark reception building, I thought about my first few weeks with Uncle Sam.

Stumbling off the bus that first night at Fort McClellan, in Alabama, I had been welcomed by a grim-faced drill sergeant. Even though we had been on a plane for hours and had then been taken on a long bus ride, about forty of us were marched into the mess hall for a meal. It was well past midnight. After our meal, we sat through a long film introducing us to the Women's Army Corp. Finally, exhausted, we were given sheets and allowed to make up our bunks. I had barely fallen asleep with I was jerked awake by a glaring light and loud voices. Ordered to bring a blanket and one pillow, I had stumbled down into a dark basement. It was a tornado alert.

That had been the beginning of the six longest weeks of my life. Basic training was just like living at home with Daddy. Every minute of every day was planned. I marched, drilled, and got up at five every morning. I was given several types of uniforms and I had to iron them three or four times a day. I scrubbed and cleaned, polished boots, made beds, and learned how to use an M-16 automatic rifle. When one member of the platoon messed up, we all paid the price. I learned how to fold my clothes according to army regulation, how to pass daily inspections, and sat through eight hours of classes every day. Unfortunately, I had landed in the "fuck up" platoon, where the mass punishments meted out felt just like Daddy's. We could never seem to please our grim, unhappy drill sergeant. I was happy when the whole terrible mess was over, and I was finally sent to AIT.

AIT stood for Advanced Individual Training, and I was now at Fort Jackson, in South Carolina. Janet and I would be trained to become Food Service Specialist's. As we stumbled into the reception building, I was glad to see the sergeant on duty. I was tired enough to lie on the floor and sleep forever. We were assigned rooms and allowed to go to bed.

A knock on the door roused me from deep sleep. Opening my eyes, I squinted at my watch in the gray dawn. Janet stirred in the bed next to me, and called out sleepily, "We didn't get in until 2:00 this morning."

"First Sergeant wants you women in his office right away!" a firm voice answered.

Groaning, I struggled from bed and fumbled for my clothes. I sometimes regretted my decision to join the army. I was getting pretty tired of the discipline and rules. In the six weeks I had been in the army, I had seen Gary only once. In basic training, we had not been allowed to stay off post overnight. Gary and I had stayed in the guest house and we had seen each other during daylight hours only. Now that I was at AIT, I was hoping I would see him more often.

Janet and I knocked on the First Sergeant's door. Reporting in, we were greeted and given our orientation speech. We learned that on our first weekend, we would not be allowed off post, but on the following weekends we could go where we pleased. We were given uniforms and a schedule for classes. Classes would have men and women together. The First Sergeant told us we were lucky to be part of Echo Company. In Delta, we were told, the women ran three miles every day.

Armed with this information, Janet and I began our training. We were split up and assigned new roommates. I liked Casey, my new roommate, and I liked class. There were only five women in my class, so I received a lot of attention from the male students. I liked that a lot. Naturally, I told myself, since I'm married, I can't even think of fooling around. Sometimes, as I confided to my roommate, I found myself regretting my marriage. She seemed to understand and confided that she had refused to marry her boyfriend because she felt she was too young. I envied her freedom to date the many men available on the base.

I found myself especially attracted to a tall, good-looking black man called Preacher.

"Hi, Lady," Preacher said on the second day of class, "you look beautiful today."

I blushed furiously, "How could I?" I asked, "I've got my hair up and I'm wearing these big, old cook whites."

"Hey," Preacher said seriously, "I can tell something beautiful when I see it."

"Thank you," I said simply. His compliment fed me as water to a starving plant in the desert.

Preacher was a fascinating man. He had grown up in Chicago and had been a gang member from the time he was ten years old. He claimed to have killed a man. I didn't know if I believed him, but I was drawn to him because he was exciting, tough, and the leader of our class. He told me he got into the army because he needed to make a living, and the ghetto didn't offer many chances.

He intrigued me, and, almost against my will, I found myself increasingly drawn to him. He and I worked at the same workstation and we were always together on breaks. When he invited me out for a beer, I really wanted to go.

"You know I'm married," I told him.

"Hey," he said, "it's only a beer."

We went to the club for enlisted men and, before I knew it, we were slow dancing and swaying dreamily to the music. The beer was making me feel good.

From then on, Preacher began a campaign to make love to me. I often caught him watching me intently in class. His steady brown eyes made me melt inside. I began to believe that I loved him. He was considerate of me always, spending a great deal of time at my side. We began to spend all our free time together, often going to the enlisted club to drink beer and dance. On one such occasion I relaxed in his arms as we moved to the music.

"I wish we had some weed," I murmured.

"You like weed?" he asked, pulling away from me. "That's cool! I've got some."

"Well, great! We should get together and get high sometime," I said.

"Baby, if you spend the night with me tonight, we can get high all you want," he told me, stroking my hair.

I pulled away from him. "Tonight?" I asked, my voice quavering.

"Tonight," he said firmly. "You know I love you."

"If you love me, how come you went to Chicago last weekend? You went to see your girlfriend!" I accused him jealously.

"Hey, that girl is my heart. One of my enemies shot her in the stomach. I had to go. I had to take care of him, and I did. He'll never shoot anyone again. Besides, you have a husband. My girlfriend and your husband have nothing to do with us. We're here, the music is playing, I want you and you want me. We love each other."

"I'm afraid you won't love me after it's all over," I admitted to him.

"I'll always love you," he replied firmly.

I was tempted. "You know," I said painfully, "Gary was supposed to come here this weekend. I really do miss him."

"I'm here, even if Gary isn't," Preacher replied softly.

Together, we left the club. Preacher had a motel room off post. He flagged a cab and gave the driver a name. Soon we pulled up in front of a bright neon sign. Paying the driver, Preacher pulled me from the cab, and I followed him to an upstairs room.

"Do you always keep this room?" I questioned him.

"Hey, I like my weekends off post. Anything wrong with that?"

"No," I had to agree.

Preacher reached into the drawer of a nightstand and pulled out his stash. I sat on the bed and watched him roll a joint. Soon we were both feeling mellow. It was my first high in over five months, and it hit me hard. I looked at Preacher. When his eyes met mine, I saw his desire. I wanted him, too. My Catholic conscience screamed that it was adultery, but I didn't fight the feelings. We came together and he kissed me. When he began to remove my clothes, I lay back but didn't resist. He quickly undressed.

When I saw how big he was, I panicked. I had never been with anyone so large.

"I can't handle that!" I gasped in fear.

"Sure, you can," he soothed me, "just wait."

It was horrible. I felt like I was splitting open. The pain jabbed up into my abdomen and I stifled a scream. In a few minutes it was over, and Preacher rolled off me, well satisfied. As he smoked a cigarette, I tried to come to terms with what I had done.

I had cheated on my husband.

It hadn't been worth it. Shame washed over me, and I hated myself. Why hadn't I said no? Why didn't I stop Preacher when it was hurting me so much? I had allowed him to violate me.

Engulfed in misery, I took the lonely cab ride back to post. Tears slid down my face. I knew I could never tell Gary what I had done. Worst of all, I didn't even understand why I had done it.

"Please God," I begged out loud, "please, help me never to do this again."

CHAPTER TWENTY-NINE
EL PASO

The midday sun shimmered over the barren yellow mountains. Heat danced in waves above the dusty, busy city. I had never felt such heat. It scorched like a blast form a fiery furnace. The wind whipped my hair as I followed the sergeant into the reception building.

"Welcome to El Paso," he said, giving my hand a limp squeeze. He then turned smartly on his heel and left.

A bored E4 directed me to my room, where I showered and fell into bed. I was so tired that I didn't care if it was still daylight.

Early the next morning, I began processing for my new duty station, as the first female cook to arrive at Fort Bliss. I met the Mess Sergeant and was given a hurried orientation. In two days', time, I would begin my duties as cook in the mess hall.

I spent the next two days apartment hunting. Gary wanted to live off post and I wanted to have a place ready when he arrived. I finally found a decent apartment close to post. It was furnished so I could begin living there right away if I wanted. I spent a few dollars at a thrift store for some much-needed dishes, pots and pans. When I reported for my first day at work, my little house was ready to live in.

Sgt. Rockford, the Mess Sergeant, assigned me to Shift Leader Specialist Dunden. I was the only woman in the kitchen, and I worked hard. In a few days, I had won the respect of my co-workers because I pulled my own weight. I was amused when the guys began to compete for my attention. Jose, a handsome Latin man, invited me to a party. I agreed to think about it if Gary were in town.

Two weeks later, Gary arrived. We kissed in a passionate reunion, and I promised myself our marriage would be better than ever. This was our first time together in over six months. I swore Gary and I would never be separated again. Proudly escorting him to the mess hall, I introduced him to my new friends. I quickly saw that my co-workers did not think much of my husband.

"He's not what I expected," Dunden told me privately. "You talked about the guy like he was superman!"

"It doesn't matter what you think," I replied. "In my eyes he is superman!"

That night I tossed restlessly in bed. I began to dream I was with Daddy. We were alone in a motel room.

Splash! Daddy poured wine into glasses. I took mine and lifted it to toast him, our eyes meeting in a secret smile.

"Here's to tonight," I said softly.

"Here's to my beautiful daughter," Daddy said and then pulled me into his arms and kissed me slowly on the mouth. I tasted his tongue.

"I'm glad we got away from Mommy," I said, pulling away from Daddy, and beginning to unbutton my dress. Desire was hot within me.

"She had to work," Daddy murmured, his small eyes on my bare breasts, "come here."

"Spank me, Daddy," I said. Excitedly, I lay across his lap as he paddled my bare bottom. With each smack, the area between my legs became hotter and hotter. Finally, I could hold back no longer.

Shuddering, I jerked upright in bed.

Hot shame flooded my soul, as I covered my face with my hands. Gary stirred beside me but did not waken. I hated the dream, that memory I had tried so hard to block from my mind! I was horribly ashamed of my perverted dreams. I tried so hard not to have them, to pretend that they did not exist. It was twisted to dream about my father. My dream memory of the motel scene was only one of many. Bitterly, I remembered wanting Mommy out of the way so I could be alone with Daddy. Tears filled my eyes and splashed down my face even as Gary continued to sleep beside me. I lay down and tried to feel safe. I was married now. Daddy was thousands of miles away, and I knew he could never touch me again.

The next morning found me working in the mess hall as usual when Jose reminded me of the party.

"I'd love to," I said, "count us in."

What I didn't count on was Gary's reaction.

"Come on, Baby," I coaxed, "you'll see, it'll be fun!"

His jaw set. "Stop nagging, woman! I said I didn't want to go!"

"Well, I'm going," I flared back, "even if you don't!"

Dundun's horn sounded in the driveway. He had offered to give us a ride to the party. I grabbed my purse and started out the door. Gary followed me. I pasted a smile on my face as I climbed in the front seat beside Dunden.

"Hi!" I said brightly.

"Hi, Chris," Dunden nodded to Gary as he wedged himself into the front seat. Gary took my hand and held it firmly in his. I pulled loose and turned my attention to the back seat. A handsome black man with a nice smile winked at me. I had seen him around the mess hall. I thought he was the best-looking man I had ever seen. His skin was a warm brown with red highlights, and his black, glossy hair curled in ringlets.

"Chris, you know Hawthorne, don't you?" Dunden asked.

"Sure, I do," I said, "you're the other shift leader, right?"

"Yeah." Hawthorne smiled showing even, white teeth.

We arrived at the party, and I followed Dunden inside. Several people were already drinking and dancing. After my second drink, I was high. As I joked and enjoyed the company of my friends, I noticed Gary was sullen and silent.

"Let's dance," I whispered to him.

"I want to go home!" he snapped.

I sighed. "Gary, let's not argue. Can't you just try to enjoy yourself?"

"I want to go home, now!" Gary insisted.

I went to find Dunden. "I'm awfully sorry," I told him, "but we have to go home. We have something to do."

I knew Dunden saw through my excuses, but he didn't say anything. He picked up his car keys and jerked his head toward the door. "Let's go," he said.

"Hey," Hawthorne came up behind us, "I'll catch a ride with you."

Riding home, Gary and I sat in the back seat with Hawthorne. I was brooding and quiet, listening to a love song playing on the radio. Hawthorne picked up the tune and began to sing along. He had an unusually fine voice.

"I like the way you sing," I turned to him. "What's your first name, anyway?"

"Charles," his smile was heart melting.

Gary gave my hand a sharp jerk. I lapsed once again into silence. Furious with Gary for spoiling my evening, I pulled my hand from his and edged away from him. I closed my eyes and leaned my head against the seat. Silent, I listened as Charles sang softly with the radio.

CHAPTER THIRTY
CRACKS IN THE WALL

I straightened my aching back. Baking cookies was hard work. Shoving my hair out of my eyes, I grinned at Victor who smiled back, showing his white teeth. My heart raced. He was very, very, cute. Almost unwillingly, I admitted to myself that I liked him.

"Hey," I said softly, "that acid you got for me and Gary was no good, man. We didn't get high at all."

"Yeah, I know," Victor agreed, "me and Jimmy tried some. It was just no good. I hate that we wasted our money."

"That's okay," I shrugged, "it goes that way sometimes."

"What did Gary say?" Victor asked.

I laughed. "He said, far out, man. I don't feel nothing!"

Victor laughed with me, "That's a trip."

"Do these cookies look okay?" Victor was training me to replace him as baker in the mess hall, since he had to ship for Korea soon.

"They look beautiful," Victor stood close to me, "just like you!"

"Thanks," I blushed.

Dunden interrupted our conversation. "Chris, come clean the grill, you're not the baker yet!"

"Okay." I rinsed my hands and approached the grill. Scraping it down, I tossed hot water on it as I had been taught. "Oops!" I muttered I had forgotten to empty the grease pan under the grill. Grabbing the grease bucket, I stooped to pull out the little drawer that collected the hot fluid. All at once, hot grease splashed over the top of the drawer and spilled on my pants, burning painfully. I drew back with a cry of pain.

"What's wrong?" Hawthorne was at my side.

"Oh, I did something stupid," I said. "I spilled grease on myself."

"Here," gently, he thrust me away from the grill, "let me show you how to clean it."

I watched him clean that greasy, burned grill in the space of a few minutes. He finished it off by rubbing a slice of lemon across it to make it shine.

"You did a terrific job!" I said, impressed, "thank you!"

"No problem," Hawthorne said. He turned and walked from the room. I watched his retreating back thinking how nice Hawthorne was.

Later, I was shining up the service line when Sgt. Rockford called me. I dropped the cleaning cloth and went to see what he wanted.

"Yes, Sgt.?" I asked.

Sgt. Rockford was standing with Hawthorne. "I need two cooks," he said, "to work the cook-out tomorrow. I'm sending you and Hawthorne. That way I have one black and one white, one male and one female."

"Okay," I said. "What do I have to do?"

"Just follow my lead, I'll show you," Hawthorne told me.

Early the next morning, Sgt. Rockford drove to the cook-out area. I rode with him and brought along a change of clothes. Once the meat was cooking, I would change from my military whites. Hawthorne was already working when we arrived. He had the grill going and the odor of cooking meat filled the air.

"Hey," Hawthorne welcomed me, "have a beer!"

"Thanks," I said, taking one, "but I'm supposed to be helping you, remember?"

"Aww, sit down and be comfortable," Charles told me.

"But I'm not comfortable doing nothing," I objected.

"You can help me later on," Hawthorne said.

I was about to answer when I saw Victor from the corner of my eye. I stood and waved to him. He was with Ross, another of the sergeants assigned to the mess hall. Victor smiled as they came up to me.

"There you are!" He turned to Hawthorne, "Hawthorne, man, are you working her?"

"No, no," I jumped in hastily, "he won't let me do anything."

Victor looked into my eyes. "We came to take you for a ride."

"I can't go," I told him. "I'm supposed to be working."

"Let her go, Hawthorne," Victor turned again to Charles, "you can handle this job."

"It's okay with me," Charles said, "Rockford's the one who brought her out here."

"I don't want to get into trouble," I said.

"Come on," Ross said, "Rockford's already drunk. He doesn't care what you do."

"Let me change clothes," I said.

Victor and Ross escorted me to the ladies' latrine, and I hurried inside to change, my insides quivering in anticipation. I forgot about Gary waiting for me at home. The beer I had drunk made me slightly lightheaded, and all I could think of was Victor waiting outside.

We got into Ross's car, and he eased it out of the crowded lot. I waved to Hawthorne as we left.

"We'll come back for you!" I promised him.

"You better!" he replied.

"You guys better remember we promised to come back for him," I told Victor.

He popped the top on a can of beer and handed it to me. "Don't worry about Hawthorne," he said, "he can take care of himself."

I nestled in the seat next to him and drank my beer. He was solid and warm, and I felt very secure. Victor put his hand under my chin and tipped my head back. As he looked into my eyes, my pulse hammered, and my breath quickened. Ross chuckled beside us. "What are you guys doing, man?"

"Nothing!" I said quickly. "I'm married, remember? We didn't do anything!"

"Yeah, you're married," Victor said, "but I don't think you have much of a marriage."

I pulled away from him. "What do you mean?" my voice scaled up several notches, "I have a good marriage!"

"That punk is no good!" Ross said somberly.

"How can you say that?" I cried, "You don't even know him!"

"We got eyes," Ross said, "we can see how he treats you. The guy's a little creep. He hangs on you, drags you down. He thinks he owns you, man."

I began to cry. The things Ross was saying hit too close to home. My carefully constructed fantasy was crumbling around me.

"If you stay with this guy," Ross was still talking, "you're gonna end up supporting him. I bet you were taking care of him before you joined the army."

I couldn't speak so I just nodded.

"Jesus, I didn't mean to make you cry," Ross said.

Victor gently stroked my hair. It didn't occur to me that he might have an ulterior motive in comforting me. "We all know what you were like before he got here," he told me softly. "You were happy, you smiled all the time. Now, you're worried looking. You never smile anymore. He walks into the mess hall and you change. You get all tense and nervous. That isn't any good."

I wiped away tears with the palms of both hands. "No, I guess it isn't."

Victor held my hand in his, "It's no good fooling yourself."

I drew a shuddering breath. "Maybe I did make a mistake," I admitted, "but I don't see how I can leave him. He needs me, he's lost without me."

"Yeah, he needs you," Ross sneered, "what the guy needs is a Mommy, not a wife."

I pressed both hands to my aching head. "I know I have to do something," I said, "but I don't want to talk about it anymore."

We were quiet. Victor was still holding my hand, as Ross headed the car toward the mess hall. When it stopped, he jumped out. "I need to get something," he said, hurrying inside. Victor and I got out of the car and went inside. I stood watching while Victor checked over his supplies for the next day. Suddenly, he stopped and turned to me.

"Chris," he said softly, "I love you."

My hand paused in the aimless circles I was tracing on the table. "What?" I asked stupidly.

"I love you," he said intensely. "Chris, I do. I've never felt this way about anyone before."

I looked at Victor. I could see the change in him. His eyes were pleading and sincere. I could feel his love. I believed him. I knew he loved me.

He and I left the mess hall together. Victor flagged a cab and directed the driver to his apartment. Picking up Hawthorne was forgotten. Gary was forgotten. Only Victor was there.

Later, after it was all over, and Victor put me into a cab, I tried to gather my thoughts. As the cab sped toward home, I was torn between happiness and depression. I was happy because Victor was in love with me. I was troubled because the sex had been disappointing. I hadn't enjoyed it. I had pretended to be satisfied, but sex with Victor was even more painful than sex with Gary. Uneasily, I wondered if I was normal.

I was also feeling guilty and afraid. Adultery was a sin. I admitted to myself that my marriage was over, but adultery was still wrong.

The cab stopped in front of my door. I paid the driver and slowly climbed out. Gathering my courage with both hands, I slowly turned the doorknob. Inside, Gary was waiting.

CHAPTER THIRTY-ONE
THE BREAKUP

"Gary, this is really hard," I twisted my hands together. "I only know one way to say this." I paused and took a deep breath. With his fists clenched and blue eyes like ice, Gary was angry because I was home from the cook-out so late.

"Gary, I'm in love with another man," I blurted.

"What!"

"I said, I'm in love with another man," I avoided looking into her eyes.

"I don't believe you!" That's when I looked at Gary. The blood had drained from his face leaving him paper white.

"It's true," I said unhappily. "I never wanted this to happen, but it did." I took another deep breath. "I think we should get a divorce."

"You're lying! You're fucking crazy! What are you talking about? You go to work this morning and you come home from work in love with someone else in the afternoon? What have you been doing all day, acting like a whore?" Gary caught me by both arms and shook me hard, his fingers crushing into the flesh of my arms.

"Stop, Gary! You're hurting me!" I cried.

Gary tightened his hold. "Tell me," he screamed, "what in the hell are you talking about? Who is this man? Have you been fucking him?" His blue eyes were marble hard with rage.

"Calm down!" I yelled, "I can't talk to you like this."

He threw me aside and took a deep breath of his own. "I'm calm," he said dangerously, "now tell me."

"You don't know him," I began uneasily, looking down at my feet. I felt horribly guilty. Gary didn't deserve what I was doing to him. "We work together, and his name is Victor. I didn't mean to fall in love with him, it just happened. But he made me see the truth about something. You and I are no good anymore. The truth is, Gary, I don't love you, I'm beginning to feel trapped."

A glass flew past my shoulder and crashed against the wall. I whirled around to see Gary kneeling among the shards of glass. With a shaking hand, he grasped one of the glittering slivers and slashed at his wrist. I screamed and jumped at his hand. Struggling with him, I managed to knock the sliver from his fingers. I pulled him away from the glass.

"What's wrong with you?" I screamed. "Gary, things are not that bad!"

"The hell they aren't," he sobbed, "you're not leaving me! Not ever! If you do, I swear I'll kill myself!"

"Don't say that!" I was horrified. "You can't keep me here. I'll leave if I want to. You don't own me, Gary, and you won't kill yourself either." Tears were running down my face as I headed for the door. I hated myself for what I was doing to him. A part of me still loved him. Gary grabbed me and, yanking viciously, pushed me into the bedroom. Jamming the door shut, he blocked it from the outside. I couldn't get out.

"Let me out!" I beat on the door with my fists. "Gary, let me out! You can't keep me in here! I hate you! Let me out!" I was screaming at the top of my voice.

Giving way to my feelings, I hurled against the door again and again. I screamed and swore. Somewhere, in a corner of my mind, I wondered why our neighbors didn't call the police. We were making enough noise. It sounded like Gary was killing me.

After what seemed like hours, Gary opened the bedroom door. Worn out from screaming and crying, I brushed past him into the bathroom. While I ran a bath, he pleaded with me. I ignored him; my feelings closed within me. I felt numb, and I only cared about getting away from him.

"Chrissy, please," Gary pleaded, "you can't leave me. I'll never make it without you. We can work this out, I know we can." Tears ran down his face, "you only think you love this guy."

"Leave me alone, Gary." I said tiredly. I bathed and dressed. Brushing past him again, I went out the door and to a telephone booth on the corner. Fumbling for change, I called Dunden.

"Gary and I had a fight," I told him. "Dunden, I know you're a friend. Could you come get me? I'd like to talk to you for a while."

"Where are you?" Dunden asked me.

I told him. "Wait there, I'll come and get you," he hung up the phone.

In minutes, Dunden had picked me up. As we drove past the apartment I shared with Gary, we saw him standing on the curb. Catching sight of us, Gary's eyes narrowed in anger and he let out a long shrill whistle. I knew the whistle was a signal for me to come back.

"Listen to that guy!" Dunden exclaimed, "He's whistling after you like you were a dog or something!"

Dunden and I drove around for hours while I talked. He listened carefully, nodding his head occasionally. When I finally wound down, he gently put his arm around my shoulders.

"What are you going to do?" he offered me a cigarette. I fumbled with the lighter. "I'm going to leave him," I said, blowing smoke through my nose.

"For what it's worth, I think you're making the right decision," he said. "Would you like me to take you to a motel for the night? I'll loan you the money."

I shook my head. "I have to go home. I'm not afraid to face him. Besides, he might try something crazy."

Dunden dropped me off in front of the apartment. Indescribably weary, I turned the doorknob. At that same moment, I saw Gary sitting on the side fence of the yard. His mouth drooped and his face wore a bitter expression. My heart went out to him. It hurt me to cause him so much pain.

"Is he another boyfriend?" he sneered.

"I'm leaving you, Gary," I said simply. "All I need is a couple of days to get everything straight. You can stay here, I don't care." I went into the house. Shutting the bedroom door, I undressed and dropped into bed. I heard Gary come in, but I closed my eyes and pretended to be asleep. All I wanted was rest.

CHAPTER THIRTY-TWO
CIRCLES

"He was here again," the girl said, helping herself to a cookie.

"Who was here?" I asked absently.

"Your ex," my neighbor replied. "I felt so bad for him. He was sitting on the step crying."

"Oh, God," I said, "that's all I need. Here's your sugar, Cindy."

"Thanks," she said leaving, "but I think you're awfully mean to that poor guy."

"Who cares what you think!" I muttered to myself. "You should have my problems." Looking around my prettily furnished apartment, I sighed. I was grateful to Sgt. Adams, one of the mess sergeants for helping me to find this place, but I was troubled. I knew he wanted something in return. He lived downstairs, but it was getting harder and harder to avoid him.

I had been living alone for almost a month. Not a day had passed that Gary hadn't come by the mess hall. Now he had taken to dropping by my apartment. He had even stolen the key to my apartment one day, locking me out of my own home. Again, I called on Dunden, but I knew he was getting tired of my problems.

Thinking of Dunden made me squirm. Victor had shipped for Korea two weeks before, leaving me alone and scared. In my panic I had turned to Dunden. We had a miserable one-night stand in a motel room. He had seemed so kind and helpful; we ended up in bed together almost before I knew it. The whole experience was a terrible mistake and I noticed a change in Dunden. We had lost something the old comfortable footing was gone.

I sighed. Was life ever simple? It seemed to me that I had been dealing with problems for as long as I could remember. I was tired. Being on my own was harder than I have ever imagined.

A knock on the door distracted me. I turned the knob to see Sgt. Adams standing on the step.

"Hey girl!" he greeted me. "Come on down later, some of the guys from the mess hall are dropping by for a drink."

"Okay," I said, "why not? It sounds like fun." I didn't want to be alone, anyway.

A little later I knocked on Adam's door. Sgt. Rockford had arrived, and he cradled a drink in one hand.

"Hey!" he said.

"Well, hi," I replied, "how are you?"

"I'm okay," he said. "I heard your apartment was in this complex."

"Right upstairs," I answered gaily, "do you want to see it?"

"Sure," he said smoothly.

I caught a glimpse of Adam's face as I led Rockford upstairs. He looked furious. I closed the door and, my heart pounding, I showed Rockford my compact but tasteful efficiency apartment. As I finished the brief tour, I noticed that he was staring at me.

"What's wrong?" I asked nervously.

"What did you really mean by asking me up here?" he asked softly.

"What do you mean?" I returned, "You're my boss and I wanted to be polite."

"No, baby," he caught me in two strong arms, "you meant more than that."

What did I mean? I asked myself, and what else did I expect? Naturally, he would think that I wanted to sleep with him. After all, I had invited him up. I didn't even know why. Bleakly, I wondered what I was looking for. I stood like a doll as he unhooked my bra. He guided me to the bed and took off the rest of my clothes. I lay there as he stroked and probed my bare body. When he guided my mouth to his penis, I obeyed. My brain clicked off and I was numb, simply doing what he wanted.

Afterward, I lay in his arms. As usual, I felt miserable and guilty. He glowed with pleasure as he stroked me.

"I know you love me," he said with deep satisfaction. He tipped my chin up and looked into my eyes, "Say, it," he ordered me, "say that you love me!"

"I love you," I repeated woodenly.

"I knew it. From now on, you're mine. You belong to me. You are to see only me. You got it?"

I nodded. He was old and he was married, but I felt I must obey him.

"Good," he took my hand and led it to his member. I was horrified to find him hard again. I got no sleep that night. Every time I drifted off; he woke me up for move love making. I was heavy eyed and listless at work the next morning.

"Chris, are you okay?" Charles Hawthorne asked me. "You seem out of it, girl!"

"I'm fine," I told him, forcing a smile.

The truth was I felt miserable. Repeatedly, I asked myself what I was getting into. I didn't want to be involved with Rockford, but I couldn't seem to help myself. I felt that all the men on base were talking about me. They were probably calling me a whore, tramp, or even worse names

I couldn't seem to handle being alone. I kept the lights on all night long. Evil things seemed to slither through the apartment. I tried saying the Lord's Prayer and Hail Mary's nonstop, but the prayers didn't help. I would nod off into an uneasy sleep, and jerk awake at the slightest noise. Being with Rockford was better than being alone.

Finally, the workday at the mess hall was over. Rockford had said he would not be able to come over; he had to spend the night with his wife. I was relieved but still afraid. Maybe smoking a joint will help, I thought to myself. I got my stash and rolled myself a joint. I smoked it but it didn't help; I felt more alone than ever.

Someone knocked at the door. I ran to answer it. Ross stood outside.

"Can I come in?" Ross asked.

"Sure, you can!" I cried.

"Hawthorne's in the car," he said, stepping over the threshold, "and I came to see if you want to go to Old Mexico with us."

"Oh, yes," I said, "I've never been there!"

Ross sniffed the air. "Hey! You've been smoking weed in here!"

"Just a little," I admitted.

"I don't fool with that stuff," Ross said disgustedly.

"No?" I shrugged, "Well to each his own."

"Let's get going," Ross said, starting out the door.

Tingling with anticipation, I followed him. Once I was wedged in the front seat between Ross and Hawthorne, I was happy again. I felt the evening was going to bring something good. At least I wasn't alone anymore.

CHAPTER THIRTY-THREE
OLD MEXICO

The streets glittered and rocked with excitement. The bright lights were dazzling. Every nerve tense with anticipation, my eyes seeing all the color, the excitement, I could feel the intense atmosphere. Seemingly homeless children roamed the streets, begging for pennies. Vendors hawked their wares, everything from chewing gum to rings. Enticing girlie signs lined the sidewalks, luring soldiers inside the nightclubs. Music jangled in the air. This was Mexico, alive with both the old and the new.

I took in everything. Again, wedged between Charles Hawthorne and Ross, I walked the streets. The joint I had smoked earlier deepened my perceptions as I allowed Ross to guide me into one of the clubs.

"Want a drink?" Ross loomed over me.

"Sure, why not?" I said excited. "Where's Hawthorne?"

"Sitting at the bar."

"Why doesn't he sit with us?" I asked.

"Oh, he's got things to do. He'll come over later," Ross dismissed my question.

I let it pass. I was feeling too good to let anything bother me. Dreamily, I sipped my drink. Suddenly, Ross and I were surrounded by musicians. They began to strum, and Mexican tunes filled the small club. Delighted, I turned to Ross, "Where did they come from, Sgt.?"

"Call me John," Ross was watching me intently.

"Okay, John," I said, "where did they come from?"

"They play this club, man. I asked them to play for you."

"That was nice, thank you," I smiled.

"You are welcome," Ross reached for my hand and held it.

I disentangled my hand. Something strange was going on with him.

"Hey! There's no action here!" Hawthorne was at our table. I breathed a sigh of relief. "Let's go somewhere else." He suggested.

"Okay, man," Ross agreed. We crowded back out into the street and went inside another small club. When Ross went to the bar for drinks, I grabbed Charles Hawthorne by the hand.

"Don't leave me with him, please." I whispered, "He's acting really strange. I think he wants me to fool around with him and his wife's a friend of mine. I don't want to get involved."

Charles looked at me strangely. "Okay," he said quietly.

Ross returned to the table bearing three coconut shells. "Mexican Zombies!" he beamed.

I grabbed mine and pulled through the straw. Whatever the drink was, it was potent and good. I watched the dancers through a haze.

"Want to dance?" Ross was at my elbow.

"I guess so," I said disappointedly, wanting to dance with Charles. I watched him over Ross's shoulder while we were dancing. Ross spun me around and spoke, breaking into my thoughts.

"Do you have some money I could borrow?"

"Yeah," I said slowly, "I guess I could. How much do you need?"

"I'll let you know."

We moved back to the table. "I can see you guys have eyes for each other, so I'm going to split," Ross said.

"You don't have to go," I protested.

"It's okay," he said, "you two have a good time. Chris, can I borrow that money?"

"How much?" I asked, reaching for my purse.

"Fifty?"

"Sure." I pulled out a fifty-dollar bill and handed it to him.

"Thanks, man!" Ross reached for my hand and kissed it. "See you!"

"Wait a minute!" Charles jumped up from the table and followed him to the door. It looked like the two of them were having a heavy discussion. Finally, Charles came back to the table.

"I'll get your money back for you," he promised.

"I'm pretty sure he'll pay me back. Anyway, I can spare it. I already paid my rent this month," I said.

Charles laughed, "Would you like to dance?"

"I've been waiting all night for you to ask!" I told him.

Moving into his arms, I danced dreamily. His arms tightened around me and he sang softly into my ear. I was floating. He was very tender, and I felt protected. I wasn't ready for the song to end.

We left the club, and once again, we were out on the sidewalk. I turned to Charles, "I've never been here before. I'd love to see something of Juarez."

"Okay, girl!" Charles took my hand. We passed a street vendor and I turned to look at his jewelry. "Oh, how pretty!" I exclaimed, holding up a ring with a beautiful pink stone.

"How much?" Charles asked.

While Charles and the vendor argued I looked at his other things. I exclaimed with pleasure when Charles slipped the ring on my finger. He also bought a gold cross on a chain and hung it around my neck. Suddenly turning serious, I looked him full in the eye and blushed.

"I think I'm falling in love with you," I said.

Charles shook his head. "Don't say that! You don't know what you're talking about." He led me to a curb, "Sit down and listen," he said.

"Look, girl, you're young. You've been through a few things and you're alone. There are people out there who will take advantage of you. Why do you think Ross asked you to come over here tonight?"

"But I never thought of Ross that way!" I broke in, "His wife's a friend and I'd never do anything to hurt her!"

"Ross thought you would sleep with him. Where do you think he got that idea?"

"I don't know! How could he? I'm not like that!" I cried in anger.

"Don't be so naive!" Charles said, "Do you have any idea what's being said about you all over the post? Ross says that he and Victor created a monster. All you care about is sex and you'll sleep with anyone."

"That's not fair!" I burst out. "I was involved with Victor, but I loved him! He was there for me when Gary and I split up. Dunden claimed he was in love with me, but I told him no way! I don't want to be involved with him. And Rockford, well, I don't know why I slept with him. I guess I was alone and scared. But I don't want to have an affair with him. He's married and he's old, plus, he's my boss." I wound down slowly.

"Look," Charles said reasonably, "you don't have to say yes to everyone. You can say no."

"I wish it was that easy. Maybe you could say no or someone else could say no, but I can't. In my heart I want to, but I can't get the word out. Everything's all mixed up and I know I'm messed up." I paused for breath. "I really am trying to get my head together."

"Come on," Charles pulled me to my feet.

"Where?"

"I have to get you home."

"How?" I asked, "Ross left us."

"I'll get a cab," he said easily.

"Why did you come here tonight?" I asked, suddenly curious.

"You want the real reason?"

"Yes."

"I came to buy some sex."

"Oh," I felt myself blushing. "I guess I spoiled your plans. I'm sorry."

We began to walk along the street. "You could spend the night with me," I said softly.

"No strings?" Charles asked, watching me. "I'm not going to promise that I'll stay past tonight. I'm not going to promise to fall in love with you. I don't need any complications in my life right now."

"No strings," I promised. Charles flagged down a passing taxi and we got inside. Inside the warm cab he pulled me into his arms and something inside me clicked. Tonight, I would not sleep alone and, maybe, just maybe, something more would come of this friendship. Charles was the sincerest person I had met in a long time. I felt he cared.

"You're so pretty," he said kissing me. "And I can see why Victor fell in love with you. You sure have some soft skin."

"Thank you," I whispered.

The silence was broken only by our kiss. I couldn't wait to get home.

CHAPTER THIRTY-FOUR
CONFRONTAION

That night in Mexico turned into a life commitment between Christine Anderson and Charles Hawthorne. By the time we had been living together for four months, I was pregnant. My emotions were mixed. Naturally, I would have my baby, but I was uncertain about Charles. I wasn't sure he loved me. He was an independent man who wanted no restrictions on his life. He liked to come and go as he pleased. I was surprised when he woke me one night to tell me he loved me. Overcome with emotion, I wanted to be sure that he meant it.

"You're not telling me this just because I'm pregnant?" I had to know.

"I love you, Chrissy, I mean it." I couldn't doubt the sincerity in his brown eyes.

We were married in December. I was discharged from the army and our baby was due in June. My divorce from Gary was final only shortly before Charles and I were married.

We named our baby Charles Junior. When he was about two months old, Mommy flew to El Paso to visit us. This was her first time to see the baby, and she held him close, covering his little face with kisses.

"I always knew you'd make a good mother," she said, tucking him securely into his little crib.

Turning to face me, she gave me a long, hard look. I could see something was on her mind.

"Come and sit down," she said. Sitting side by side on the couch, she took my hand and held it for a moment. "Such little hands," she said tenderly, "and such a slender body to have worked so hard in your lifetime. I flew here determined to talk to you. You are a grown woman now, with a family of your own. I want to know something." She paused and took a deep breath. "I have always suspected that Daddy had a sexual relationship with you. Is it true? Did your father have sex with you? I want to know if I've been crazy all these years."

I sat there, stunned. Thoughts whirled through my mind. My goal had always been to protect her. I didn't know exactly what her suspicions were, and I groped for a way to answer her.

"I always suspected there was something going on between you and your father. If you recall, you'll remember that I asked you more then once after you turned sixteen." She rose and walked across the room, rubbing her arms with her hands, "I confronted him, you know, and he swore I was crazy. He threatened to have me committed."

I twisted my coffee cup in my hands. Poor Mommy, to have lived with her suspicions all these years. I knew what it felt like to be threatened by Daddy. I knew what it was to be afraid of him.

"Do you remember when I was eleven?" I asked her. "I came to you, then. I told you that he woke me up one night, fondling my breasts."

Mommy closed her eyes as though in great pain. "I remember," she said softly, "I questioned him. He said you were having a sexual fantasy about him."

I looked at her amazed. "Sexual fantasy! At eleven years old? I didn't even know what a sexual fantasy was! Did you really believe I would make something like that up?" It hurt to think she could believe that I would tell such a lie.

Mommy sighed again. "I didn't know what to believe. I wanted to believe him. I guess I convinced myself what he said about you was true. I had to believe him. I had all you kids, no education, and no place to go."

"I really wish you had believed me," I said quietly. A great painful lump filled my throat. I choked down the impulse to cry.

Mommy did not notice my distress and continued in a rush, "Underneath, I always suspected something was going on. Now, he acts like he wants Tracey."

"Oh, no," I said slowly, "I hate to hear that. I always tried to protect Tracey and Anne. Somehow, I hoped they would escape."

"Escape what, Chrissy? I think it's time you told me everything."

I squirmed uncomfortably. "Daddy fondled me for years. He touched my private area and forced me to have oral sex with him." That was all I could bring myself to tell her. I just couldn't tell her the whole truth. Inside, I was still afraid of driving her over the edge of sanity. She seemed to have such a fragile hold on reality. I was afraid she would condemn me. She might stop loving me if I told her the whole truth.

"Why didn't you tell me? I would have believed you if you had come to me again."

"Daddy threatened me. He said you would have a complete mental breakdown and it would be my fault. I believed him. I couldn't tell you. I was afraid of what it would do to you."

"Your grandfather molested me when I was small," Mommy told me now. "I never got over it. I almost grew to hate him. To this day, I don't like being alone with him." She paused for a moment. "Your grandmother doesn't know. I never told her."

I nodded, not surprised at this news. I seemed to have always known it. "I think Daddy told me about it," I said quietly.

"And now he's after Tracey! I know it's the truth. I could bet my life on it. He's the cruelest man I've ever known. He's ruined my life. All the surgery I've had, all the sickness, has been his fault. The human body can only stand so much pain." She took my face in her hands, "My poor, Chrissy, how much you've had to bear! Too much for a child. Your childhood was taken from you; you grew up much too fast." She heaved a huge sigh, "But it wasn't my fault!" she finished. She looked away but not before I saw a glimmer of tears in her eyes.

I tried to absorb the fact that the secret was out. I had guarded this knowledge, to protect her, my whole life. Now she knew. What would she do with the information? I was pulled from my reflections by her voice.

"You're happy now, aren't you?"

I could hear the hope and the agony in her voice. I would not take that hope away. "Yes, Mommy," I said gently. I would not add to her pain.

CHAPTER THIRTY-FIVE
CHURCH

I followed Charles through the front door, taking in my new home in one quick glance. The small living room, the hallway, and the bedrooms were covered with pretty, light paneling. Under an accumulation of dirt, the floors were bright linoleum. The house was new and solid, but it needed an airing. As I followed Charles on the grand tour, our baby wiggled in my arms. Absently, I shifted his weight. I felt dazed. Things were moving too fast. I was a wife again, and a mother. I had a new home, a new family, and a new state to adjust to. Charles had a kind family, but nothing could alter the fact that I was here, in Gurdon, Arkansas.

"Be back in a minute," Charles broke into my thoughts. "Here," using a rag he scrubbed a clean place on the floor, "sit down and rest."

Gratefully, I slid to the floor. Charles Junior, four months old, was quiet in my arms. Looking around my new house, I felt a little proud. This was the first home I could really call my own.

A short while ago, Charles' discharge from the army had become effective. It had always been his dream to own a home in his hometown, so we had purchased this little house shortly before his discharge. I felt a little dazed, but proud. Owning a home had been a dream of mine, too.

So here I was with my new husband, new baby, and a whole new family. I didn't feel unwanted because Fanny, my mother-in-law, and Betty, my husband's sister, had made me feel welcome.

"Come on, Chris," I started. Charles stood in the door. "We've got a lot to do."

The next few days were busy with moving. We had to buy furniture and a bed for the baby's room. Once the fury of moving was over, however, my life became very quiet. Charles was working and I stayed home with the baby every day. Daily walks to the library and my mother-in-law's house were my only diversions.

"What's wrong with you, girl?" Charles asked one night, annoyed. "Stop that pacing!"

"I'm bored," I said plaintively. "You don't know! You work all day and you're out every single night! I don't have anything to do!"

"I'm only playing cards," Charles said mildly.

To please me, Charles began to take me to an occasional party. We would leave the baby with his cousin and stay out all night drinking and dancing. I loved the jukes, the music and the drinks, but still I was restless.

Mama, as I called Charles's mother, did not appear to have my problem with boredom. She stayed home every day and seemed to be happy. I liked being around her. She was contented and I envied her.

Just to have a new place to go, I accepted Mama's invitation to visit her church. This would be my first experience with a Black church. I was excited, but apprehensive. I couldn't understand why black people went to one church and white people to another. When I asked Charles about it, he just shrugged.

"You live in Arkansas, now," he told me. "There are a lot of things black people and white people do separately. I even graduated from an all-black school, and that was in 1965."

I was aware of subtle differences. "I know we get stared at a lot in town," I agreed, "but it seems like people could come together for church. I really can't understand why they wouldn't."

On Sunday morning, I carefully chose a green dress from my closet. I took rollers from my long hair and brushed it around my shoulders. I was nervous when I left the house and walked the short distance to church. Grabbing my courage with both hands, I mounted the steps and stepped inside. A pretty, black lady handed me a program and gave me a hug. Pleased, I hugged her back.

"Here, darlin, come on," Mama was at my side. She guided me to a pew in front. In a moment, I was surrounded by people. They shook my hands, hugged me, and covered my cheeks with kisses. The pastor grabbed my hand and pumped it vigorously. I was overcome. I felt as though my thirsty and parched emotions were being watered and revived with loving care. I had never felt so loved or so welcome.

When the service began, I was spellbound. Nothing in the Catholic Church had prepared me for this. People were clapping their hands in church. When the choir stood to sing, I was thrilled. Never had I heard such beautiful voices. The face of the soloist was rapt.

Afterwards, walking home, I felt thoughtful and I wanted to be part that wonderful choir. Taking a deep breath of fresh air, I smiled.

CHAPTER THIRTY- SEVEN
THE APOLOGY

    The kitchen seemed coldly bright when we returned. Laughing and talking, my brother Tommy, Charles and I straggled though the front door. It had been a wonderful evening. Our little family reunion was off to a great start. I wasn't thinking about Mommy and Daddy going through a divorce, with Daddy now living in California, and Mommy living in upstate New York. I was grateful to be given a second chance to have a relationship with my family.

    I had forgotten about the uneasy telephone call from Jill, my mother's roommate that had caused me to cancel my summer classes and fly to New York. Jill had hinted that Mommy had been acting strangely. When Mommy and her new boyfriend Colby had met me at the airport, she had seemed delighted to see me, and had used the occasion to organize a family reunion.

    As I now entered the kitchen, I was totally unprepared for the sight that met my eyes. Mommy was crouched on the floor by the yellow wall phone, speaking into the receiver, but her posture seemed very odd. Tommy went upstairs, but feeling somewhat uneasy, Charles and I stayed in the kitchen. I wanted to find out who Mommy was talking to.

    "Mommy?" I questioned her softly. I walked to her and placed my hand on her shoulder. Mommy's eyes were blank, and she was babbling. With a sad horror, I realized she didn't know who I was. For a moment, my skin crawled. I gently pried the phone from her fingers and handed it to Charles. I took both her hands and held them, hard. Her eyes began to focus on me, and slowly, slowly, the nonsense words stopped dribbling from her mouth. She looked painfully sad.

    "He hates me," she said, her eyes filling with tears. "He wants me to die."

    "Nobody wants you to die," my own eyes filled, and tears ran down my face as I shared in her misery. Charles gripped my arm and shook his head. His brown eyes held a look of deep fear.

"I won't have her upsetting you," he said firmly. "I don't ever want to see you go through something like this. I want you to keep a firm grip on reality. I love you too much to see you in this kind of pain."

Grateful for his love and support, I leaned over and kissed him. "You never have to worry," I told him softly, "I'm not like her. I'm much stronger, I always have been." I looked at Mommy. I still held her hands firmly in my own. "I've got to take care of her now."

Charles handed me the phone he still held in his free hand. "I'll help you upstairs, Mercy," he told my mother gently.

Mommy looked from Charles to me, "Charles understands my pain," she sobbed.

"Why do you say that?" I asked her, surprised.

"Because he's black!" Mommy continued sobbing as Charles gently helped her up the stairs. Watching them, I dashed tears from my own eyes. Remembering that I still held the phone, I spoke into the receiver.

"Who is this?"

"Christine." The familiar fear grabbed me as I recognized my father's voice. I swayed on my feet.

"Daddy," I squeaked the childhood name in a little girl voice. I made a desperate effort to steady myself. "Charles is taking Mommy upstairs. I think she needs to go to bed."

"I think she should." Abruptly, dial tone buzzed in my ear, and I realized that Daddy had broken the connection. Shaken, I went to help Charles. Together we put Mommy to bed. The blank stare had returned, and she sobbed as though her heart would break. She called brokenly for Colby, declaring her love for this man who had come into her life after she and Daddy separated. I sat quietly beside her, stroking her hair until she fell asleep.

I thought about other evenings when I had walked into the kitchen to find her talking on the phone. She would be speaking earnestly, often tearfully, as though to someone important but when I would ease the phone from her hand, only buzzing dial tone met my ear. Her mental condition was getting worse and I was worried.

I didn't like her roommate situation. I had awakened several times in the night to strange noises in the hallway. Peeking out the bedroom door, I was amazed to see Jill running naked through the hall and up and down the stairs. Since she had moved into the house both Mommy and Anne had taken to sleeping in the nude. Something in the house seemed strange and out of place.

Finally, now, Mommy was sleeping soundly. As I softly descended the stairs, the phone rang. I grabbed it quickly.

"Hello," I said softly, not wanting to wake her

"Christine," it was my father. I shivered and looked over my shoulder. I felt he was in the room with me.

"Yes, Daddy," I controlled the tremor in my voice determined to sound more adult. His next words shocked me.

"You've told your mother about us," he said abruptly. "I know this." Unspoken between us lay the old threat. I had told and she had gone crazy. Purposely, I pushed the guilt out of my mind. It was not my fault. I did not cause my mother's mental breakdown. I prepared words to defend myself from my father's attack. His next sentence shocked me.

"Will you forgive me?" he asked, breaking the heavy silence between us.

"Oh, Daddy," my throat swelled. For just a moment, I was his little dark eyed girl. My heart cried out for his approval, for his love. I framed my answer with love and need. "Yes, I forgive you. I forgave you long ago. I love you, Daddy."

"I forgive you, too." As suddenly as he called, he was gone. I stared at the empty receiver. What was there for him to forgive? Guilt raised heavy in my chest, pushed into my throat, and almost choked me with its intensity. I was bad. I had tempted and seduced him. I must share equal responsibility with him for the others in my mind accused and condemned me. As I listened to the voices that spoke in my head, I slowly felt crazy. This wasn't the first time the voices had spoken. Somehow, I felt as if I had been hearing them my whole life. I didn't know then that the trauma in my life had caused me to form the fragmented state of Dissociative Identity Disorder. There were several personalities living within me.

"Wicked!" spat Caroline " You were always wicked Christine"!

Peggy nodded in solemn agreement.

"Daddy told you never to tell "

lizbeth who had been stirring within me turned her small tear streaked face to the wall.

"Lonely, want Mommy," she cried.

Maybe, Daddy was trying to apologize. Maybe it was the only way he could bring himself to an apology. Maybe, in his mind, I was equally guilty. Maybe he had to believe in my guilt. I didn't know. I only knew that I must find a way to live with my own pain. I must find a way to prove my own innocence. I could not live the rest of my life with the guilt accusing me. I could not live with the shame. I must find a way to wholeness, not for Daddy's sake or Mommy's, but for my own and (although I was unaware at the time) for all the others who lived inside me. The others who confused me because I thought I must be making them up in my need to get better. The others who puzzled and threatened me.

CHAPTER THIRTY-EIGHT
SEEKING HEALING

"Dear God" Victoria, an adult 'alter' prayed, "you know how I hurt. You know how hard I've fought to forget my past, to leave it behind me. Can't you get Chris to do anything about it? The hurt is always there, and I hate myself! I can't hold a job, or be a good wife and mother, or do anything right! I'm terrified to face each day; my insides shrivel with dread and fear. Where should I go? What should I do? I know there are things in me that need to be made right, but I don't know how to do it!"

Did God hear? Did He even care? Victoria paced around our small townhouse struggling with my past. Victoria spoke for me. I was in a depression that was so severe I had been unable to go to work for the past three days. All I did was lie on my bed and cry. The crying had triggered Victoria to come out. I could not understand why I was so depressed. Fear crippled me. The load had become too heavy for me to bear. I felt like a drowning woman, grabbing at straws. Any moment I would go under, never to come back up again. Victoria gave me a much-needed break. I was able to slip inside of the crystal cave and rest. The crystal cave was my inner world where I went when I was overwhelmed. Victoria kept pacing. My past kept impacting her present. I had so much, I should be happy! I had the home I had always wanted, a normal, healthy son and a loving husband. We had relocated to Los Angeles and left most of the racial and discrimination problems behind us in Arkansas. I felt I had a relationship with God. If I have so much, I thought in agony, why is there this big, black hole in the middle of my heart? I feel like I don't have me, I don't even know who I am! I'm afraid to go to work, and I'm afraid to stay home. I'm afraid of people. I feel like a half-person, a non-person who doesn't even deserve to take up space.

Victoria called Kassi another of my adult alters. "This depression Chris is having is overwhelming and making me weak. Could you take over for me?"

Kassi nodded slowly. "Just for a little while girlie, I've got stuff to do." Victoria nodded her understanding and disappeared into the crystal cave. Kassi laughed at the idea of prayer. Prayer was for old ladies. "If anyone gets us out of this mess, it will be me! Only I have the strength and the balls!" Jack, one of my male alters whispered softly to Kassi. "It's alright if you don't pray but call somebody and talk about the pain."

I fought the idea. Who could I call? We had only recently moved to Los Angeles and we only knew a few people. I thought of the small church in inner Los Angeles we had attended a few times, but I was deeply distrustful of church people. There did not seem to be any place in the church for problems like mine. Perhaps the pastor would listen, but perhaps he would be shocked like so many other church people I had tried to talk to. I did not want to call. What would he think of me? Would he even understand? Finally, I gave into my need and dialed the telephone with shaking fingers. I was scared.

"May I speak to the pastor?" Nervously, I questioned the deep male voice that answered my call.

"This is Pastor."

"Pastor, Kassi said," this is Chris Hawthorne. "I need to talk to someone".

"That's what I'm here for. What can I do for you?"

Encouraged by his response. Kassi forced me to tell the hateful truth. Pastor this is not easy to say. Several sons of bitches sexually abused me for years. My life is in pieces, and I feel like I'm losing my mind. Can you help me?"

"You poor child," he replied softly, "tell me about it."

Kassi faded out unwilling to discuss all the trauma and I came back. For a moment I was confused. Kassi and I shared consciousness. We had been tag-teaming switching back and forth. I began to talk.

Inside the crystal cave the little ones began to whisper.

"Can we trust him?" lizbeth asked

'I don't know" kassi little replied, "he's a man and big men always hurt us."

"I don't like him, "tina little declared.

"Well, I don't trust him," sissy little said picking up her baby doll.

"We'll just have to watch for his ding-dong. If it gets hard and he tries to put in us, we'll just kick him and run away as fast as we can," kassi little said.

The others agreed this was a good plan and began to yawn. Pulling up their brightly covered blankets and their dolls they snuggled down to take a nap.

Lizbeth had one more observation "I hope Chris can take care of us"

I was amazed at all the children who lived within me. I listened to their internal conversation with a mixture of amusement and a sense of unreality. Their observations were based on my past history.

At the pastor's suggestion I joined the church right away and began to study the lessons presented to me. As I began to know the pastor better, I began to talk freely about my experiences. I had lived with memories of abuse in my life, I had blocked a great deal from myself as protection, forcing the trauma deep into my subconscious, thus giving birth to all my alters. They each possessed a part of the memory I had lost.

Unfortunately, Pastor did not treat my confidences with care. Instead he used them to seek out wounded areas in my psyche.

The Pastor rented part of a stable and kept horses. At the time I was riding a small motorcycle back and forth to work. Pastor began calling me at work. He kept inviting me to come by and see his horses on my lunch hour. At first, I refused him but after much pressure I finally gave in. When I got there his first remark was about my legs, how beautiful they were.

Then he kissed me.

I asked him if he were testing me. His answer was no. Then he kissed me again and half pushed half carried me into the motor home he owned and had driven out to the stables.

I felt paralyzed. While he slowly pulled off my clothes, I kept telling myself I could say no. But he was a big, powerful man. I just could not tell him no.

When he had finished, he handed me some paper towels to clean up with.

"What about Annette?" I asked him. Annette was his wife.

"Annette will never believe I've touched another woman. Trust me on that" ...

This was the beginning of several trips to the motor home. Each time I could not say no.

The pastor took advantage of me when I was in a very vulnerable state. He knew I had been abused and he used that knowledge to his advantage.

The reason I'm telling you this is to say be very careful whom you trust. Now, looking back, I realize I should have insisted his wife sit in on the counseling sessions. I also should have refused his phone calls.

I really believe that the healing of an incest survivor a person who has Dissociative Identity Disorder, a person who suffers from depression and anxiety is best handled by highly skilled professionals who have much experience in these fields. The truth is, it is an emotional journey that requires the support of a wise psychiatrist or psychologist. Psychotherapy is good for support and counseling as well.

You may need medications because some disorders are generated by brain malfunctional biochemistry. Depression is an illness not a weakness and it is treatable. The problem was I didn't know any of this when I started my counseling with the church. I was left with my frustration and pain and no place to take it. I tried going to different churches. I was often booked as a speaker because of my incest background and my knowledge of the Bible. I continued one counseling with my pastor and started several support groups. I self-published a book. I filled my life with a myriad of things I wanted to use to prove that I was whole.

I even went on Christian Radio to talk about my book, take answers from callers, and to encourage survivors to join a support group.

I soon found that none of it was a comfort when I awoke sweating and screaming from nightmares in the middle of the night. None of it helped when the panic snuck up on me and shook me in its ferocious jaws. None of it was enough when I would try to assert myself at work. I limped on, crippled and broken.

CHAPTER THIRTY-NINE
THE WHEEL TURNS

It was strange there, sitting by his bed in the nursing facility. He was different, all his old strength and power were gone. In their place, I saw a beaten and weak old man. It was hard to grasp that the tyrant of my childhood was gone. How unbelievable those two major strokes could have robbed him of his vitality. And yet, he could still frighten me.

He had recovered from the suicide attempt. I thought of our flight through the rainy night as we drove to Riverside, CA, in order to sit by his bed. He had overdosed on the heart medication prescribed for him by the doctor. It had been painful to see him with so many tubes running through his body. Charles and I had joined hands and prayed for him. That had been two weeks ago. Now, he was released from the hospital and living in this nursing home.

I watched his mouth work as he tried to speak from the good side. His left arm and leg hung useless. My heart contracted with pity. His keen mind still worked, but he was unable to speak his thoughts. He couldn't get into a car and drive as he loved to do. He couldn't take a brisk walk around the yard or shave himself. I ached for him.

Little Miss Fix-It, I asked myself, can you fix this too? For years, I had fixed every pain and sorrow for him by offering him the comfort of my body. But I couldn't fix this. Perhaps someday I could move beyond the point of shouldering all my father's problems. I brushed away the cobwebs of guilt and fixed my attention on Daddy.

"Your mother," he finally brought the painful words out.

I shook my head. I knew what he wanted to ask. "I haven't seen or heard from her in three years," I told him. "My letters come back marked 'address unknown' if they come back at all. Her phone was disconnected long ago. None of us kids have heard from her."

He lapsed into silence. Again, I ached for him. Mommy had obtained a divorce and disappeared. Not long after Daddy's stroke, she had sent Marvin to live with me, but that situation had not worked out. Marvin had a lot of emotional problems I couldn't deal with and he now lived with Anne in New York. Mommy seemed to have disappeared from the face of the earth.

I searched for something to say to my father.

"Charles and I are doing fine," I offered.

He smiled. I felt desperate. I was not comfortable being alone with him.

"Charles should be back in a moment," I ventured.

"Okay," he said.

"Maybe we could take you for a hamburger," I suggested.

His mouth worked and he looked frustrated. He just couldn't bring out the words he wanted to say.

Daddy," I leaned forward, intense now. There was something I wanted to say. There was so much I still needed from him. "Are you proud of me? Do you love me at all?"

His eyes filled with tears. "Very proud," he brought out slowly, "always proud you."

I nodded. He had answered my question. I didn't know if I believed him.

"   That's all I ever wanted," I said quietly, "for you to be proud of me." Tears filled my own eyes. "I love you, Dad, it's important that you know that. I always will love you."

We were quiet. Unspoken volumes lay between us. I wasn't ready to confront him. Maybe I never would be. I could not bring up the past. It was good that he knew of my love for him. I hoped that there would be time for us to build some sort of future.

I had a long way to go. It was still hard for me to see him or spend any time with him. I knew I was angry with him, but looking at this broken man in the bed, I wondered if I could ever express that anger.

For me, I knew there was hope. The future held healing. For my father, I prayed there would be time for healing. I sadly reached for his hand and a tear slid down my face. I closed my eyes in pain.

"Damn," I whispered, "why is life so hard?"

CHAPTER FORTY
PERFORMANCE AND APPROVAL

"Daddy's girl, Daddy's girl, I'm the center of Daddy's world!" Mockingly, the words to the old country tune ran through my mind. I stared at the autoharp in my lap. Softly, I strummed the strings. The autoharp brought it all back. I closed my eyes and let my mind wander backward through the years...

"Please, Daddy, I want an autoharp like Mommy's! I just know I can sing, Daddy, please let me try!" I wanted an autoharp of my own so badly. Mommy had one and she played it very well. Daddy had promised to buy me one, too. I sat in the corner of the living room floor and silently listened for hours as Mommy and Daddy sang together. Daddy strummed his guitar and Mommy played her autoharp. The microphones stood at attention on their tall silver stands. The reel to reel tape recorder hummed softly in the background. I wanted Daddy to ask me to sing. Silently, I mouthed the words. I just knew I could sing if I had the chance. I wanted to sing with my Daddy. Maybe then, he would love me the way I craved.

Daddy never asked me to sing and I never received the promised autoharp. Years later I would sing my heart out in my church choir, searching for the approval Daddy had never given me. No matter how many praises I received for a song well sung, I still felt Daddy's disapproval and rejection hovering in the background. I would never believe that I could sing.

Daddy promised to build me a playhouse of my very own. For years I planned how my dream house should look. There would be a little kitchen with a play stove and a living room with real miniature furniture. I would have a princess telephone, just like the pictures in the Montgomery Ward catalog. I would be just like the lucky little girl, pictured playing in the glossy pages. Sadly, my promised dream house was never built. Daddy never had time.

I remembered how hard I worked as a child. I cooked meals and kept the house clean. I ran bath water for my Daddy. I watched my younger brothers and sisters because Mommy was not strong enough to do it. I became my Daddy's little slave, fetching him cups of coffee, taking off his shoes and socks, serving him sexually, even dropping out of school to take care of his children. Daddy never gave me his approval. The house was never clean enough. I never worked hard enough, and my daddy said I was a selfish girl.

"My head hurts, Daddy, it hurts so badly"! I cried in pain as I experienced the first migraine headache of my eight-year-old life.

"Shut up, Christine!" Daddy roared, "how dare you snivel and whine when your Mother's so sick. No wonder she's sick! You're a goddamned selfish girl. Stop that crying and get these goddamned kids out of here! Here," he hurled two blue tablets at me, "now stop your goddamn selfish whining!" Gulping back my sobs, I picked up the tablets. I must try harder to please Daddy.

I was supposed to make the younger children be quiet and I cried loudly when my Daddy whipped me for failing. I deserved the whipping. Sometimes I slept too soundly and did not hear my baby brother crying in the night. I was scolded because I did not come quickly enough. Mommy needed all her rest. I was selfish and I did not try hard enough to help her to become well and strong.

Now, as I sat musing and stroking the strings of my autoharp, I realized that I had been a receptacle for my father's rage. I began finally to confront my anger at his death. I began to feel the rage of not ever being good enough. I thought of all the times he had told me my mother's needs were far more important than my own. I thought of all the power he had stolen from me as he violated me. I thought of how he had told me that I was not important, he did not care about my pain, he wanted nothing to stand between my mother and him. Yet he had placed me between them all those years! His power over me did not end with his death. He was dead but I was still struggling to get away from him.

Performance! How I hated the sound of that word. I could never perform enough to win his love. I imagined myself confronting him. How I wished he were not dead! I would like to sit him in a chair in front of me, look him in the eye and tell him how angry I was. I let my imagination soar. I imagined myself kicking him around the yard. I would like to kick him until he exploded. I would like to hurl him through the air and bounce him off a brick wall. I wanted to destroy his weapons, the weapons that destroyed my childhood. I wanted to stomp on his groin and to grind his penis into the dirt.

Slowly, I felt my rage draining away. Would God punish me for the hatred I was feeling toward my father? I felt fear begin to build until I realized with startling clarity that I believed a God who I now know does not exist was exactly like my Daddy.

Underlying all my fear was a deep-seated belief that I was somehow not good enough. Underneath all my performance I was waiting for a vengeful God to take his gifts away from me and leave me lonely and struggling.

I understood that I had made my father the model for God. I wanted God to accept me and to love me, but the love I felt should have come from him I now realize I could give to myself. I understood this even though my father had never given me unconditional love.

I still work hard at releasing the rage I feel toward Daddy and Mommy. I know that I never really hated them. I know that intense rage about the abuse has masked itself as hatred. In my heart I loved both my parents. At least now I can communicate with myself with honesty. I don't have to perform. I let go of childish perceptions, fears, and hurts. The process is called maturing. I don't always like it, but I wouldn't trade my journey for the world.

CHAPTER FORTY-ONE
THE CODE OF SILENCE

"Don't tell Grandmother!"

"Don't tell your father!"

"Please! Don't tell Daddy on me!"

"Don't you tell on Donald!"

"Don't tell anyone!"

"What's done in this house stays in this house!"

"This is our secret, don't tell your mother!" For years, the voices rang in my mind. From the time I was old enough to talk, "Don't tell" was drummed into my awareness. I was not to tell Grandmother when I was punished. I was not to tell my teacher what went on at home. We were not allowed to bring friends home from school, or to tell anyone where we lived. What went on at home must stay at home.

To the casual observer, our family appeared to be normal. We were the All-American family. Daddy was the firm but loving father, Mommy was the charming, if fragile, wife and mother. We were seven wonderfully polite, well-behaved children. If Daddy seemed a bit strained at times, well, everyone knew he had a sick wife to care for. If we children were a bit unkempt, if our clothes were not fresh or our hair uncombed, it could be attributed to a busy father unskilled in caring for several small children. If our shoes looked worn out and our coats frayed, Daddy was certainly not to blame. After all, Mommy's hospital bills ate up his income.

What is not so easy to explain is the reluctance of the less-than-casual observer to become involved. My brother Tommy constantly wet his pants; why didn't his teacher ever question his problem? Anne had poor bowel control as a young child. Mommy was once mortified when Anne's first grade teacher had to clean her up after an accident. Daddy had administered punishment the day before. The Sister had to have seen the ugly black welts on Anne's buttocks and legs. She must have known the child had been beaten. Why did she never question it? I vomited daily, sometimes several times a day. My teachers told one another I had a "nervous stomach." The adults around me never seemed to realize I needed help. The code of silence was in action.

When I was about twelve years old, I struck up a casual conversation with Debra, a girl who lived about a mile from our house. I was horrified when she interjected Daddy's brutality into the conversation.

"We hear ya'll screaming when your Daddy whips you," she told me with sympathy, "ya'll sure do a lot of screaming."

I looked at the ground and kicked a tuft of grass. "Yeah, he whips us sometimes," I said, my neck scorched red with embarrassment. At the time, I was anxious that Daddy might discover my friendship with Debra. He would punish me for talking with her. Now, many years later, I wonder why neighbors a mile away never interfered when they heard us screaming? The code of silence kept us in a silent prison.

The reluctance of my grandmother and teachers to become involved only reinforced this horrendous code of silence. By the time I reached my teens, the shame was locked within me. I trusted no one. Well-meaning teachers who criticized my dress and grooming only reinforced my aloneness. I most certainly wanted to be a normal teenager, but I was not normal, my life wasn't normal, and I didn't know how to be normal. Well-intentioned ladies such as the two who took me to the Salvation Army Thrift Store to "shop" only made me feel like an oddity.

It would seem that my spotty attendance in school would have caused some comment from my teachers. Only one or two of my teachers ever asked me why I missed so much school. I told my eighth-grade choir teacher my mother had a heart condition because I was ashamed to tell him she was stoned on vodka and sleeping pills, that it wasn't safe to leave her alone and that's why I missed so much school. The isolation was complete. Adults were to be feared. Any bad report passed to Daddy from a teacher would result in severe punishment. So, I was polite. For years, adults praised me for being so mature, for taking such good care of my brothers and sisters. What a wonderful little mother I was! Sister, the bus driver, the cook in the cafeteria, never guessed at the misery in my life. Neither did the kids at school.

I was so much on the outside looking in. I had only one or two friends all through school. I was strange and different, and the other kids did not want to be friends with me. They teased me without mercy, calling me ugly and buck toothed. They did not call me on the telephone or invite me to their birthday parties. One girl told me that I spent far too much time with my younger brothers and sisters. I was alone and the code of silence flourished.

So, the code of silence continued. Even within the family ranks it gripped us. Mommy taught us not to tell on one another. This was a means of self-defense, a way of protecting ourselves from pain. The taunts, slaps, beatings, and ultimately the sexual abuse I suffered at Donald's hands were sealed within me. The incest was never talked about. After the first attempt to tell Mommy about Donald and Daddy, I never again tried to tell anyone. I pretended all was well. I was good at pretending. We were, after all, The All-American Family.

Today, the All-American family continues to play "let's pretend." Many a dysfunctional family puts on a front that all is well. Yet, sexual abuse abounds. The only protection children have lies in breaking the time-honored code of silence. Those who have been sexually abused must let their stories be known. It is long past the time to shed the blanket of victims' shame that shrouds sexual abuse. Only in this way can healing began. As awareness of incest rises to the surface, other victims will find the courage to come forth. Children must be encouraged to talk when they are violated. The cycle of abuse shatters when someone finds the courage to tell. With the telling comes healing.

There is an awareness in therapy, only when victims come forth and face the horror in their lives will the shell began to crack, and healing become possible and free. Only when victims are willing to come forth and admit the truth will they be made free of the horror in their lives. With freedom comes healing and fresh hope.

CHAPTER FORTY-TWO
BITTERSWEET PIECES

As I continue to work through this journey of recovery, I acknowledge that not all my memories are bad. For me, this acknowledgment is part of what makes recovery so painful. There were some wonderful times and those wonderful memories make the horror even more difficult to understand.

It is hard to reconcile the abuser with the daddy who brought home a seven-foot Christmas tree every year. I can still see him, struggling through the front door with that tree. It was so tall that the top had to be trimmed to fit under the ceiling. Daddy worked hard to set it up just right. Decorating the tree was a family ritual. The pine smelling green perfume of the tree filled the little house to bursting.

Out would come huge boxes of lights and decorations. Mommy saved every decoration we school children made. Huge all-day lollipops were wired on the tree. The cardboard candle I made in the third grade was taped to the wall. The angel I made in fourth grade and crowned with golden hair was given a place of honor. Glass balls, garlands, homemade ornaments, were each placed in just the right spot. Mommy made a game of it, handing each of us a decoration in turn and allowing each child to choose where it should go. The manger pieces were always put under the tree along with my glass enclosed snow scene. That snow scene was pure magic. I could shake it and, child of the south that I was, I could watch the wonder of snow flying over miniature houses.

The days before Christmas were pure joy and anticipation. Every morning there were wrapped gifts placed under the tree to shake and poke. Of course, we weren't supposed to touch them, but we always did. We anticipated the coming of Santa Claus. Mommy had stacks of Christmas albums, and nap times were now happy. We were allowed to lay and listen to all the Christmas songs.

Christmas Eve had its own special rituals. Daddy made eggnog. He always spiked it with rum. I didn't care for the taste, but I like the rich way it clung to my glass. Drinking it made me feel grown up. I would stay up as late as possible on Christmas Eve. Going to sleep was difficult and I was eager for the night to pass.

We children lay in bed talking and giggling in excited whispers. It seemed like morning would never come. Donald and Mitchell were determined to stay awake to see Santa Claus. Finally, I would drift off to sleep.

I always woke before dawn on Christmas morning. Now came the hardest part of the long wait. We were not allowed to see our toys until Mommy and Daddy got up. We would bounce on our beds and talk loudly, hoping they would hear us and get up. After what seemed like hours Daddy would leave his bedroom and go into the big kitchen. Santa usually left the toys there by the big tree.

"Let's see," we would hear him say, "whose toys are these?" or sometimes he would tease us, "nothing but coal and switches out here!"

"Daddy," we would wail, "we want to come out!"

One by one he would call us out, usually starting with the youngest child. He would pause between names so that the children left in the bedroom would hear the shrieks of joy made by the younger ones. I was fairly dancing with impatience by the time he called my name.

"Chrissy!" Out I would race. Story books, dolls, coloring books, crayons, candy, the treasures went on and on. Sometimes I would get perfume and play makeup. One year I got a pair of high heel shoes. It was always the new books that thrilled me the most. I loved to read! Nothing gave me greater joy then brand-new books that belonged only to me.

After we examined our toys came the fun of opening the wrapped gifts. How glad I was that we never opened our gifts on Christmas Eve! Again, the ritual was gifts handed out by Mommy or Daddy, one at a time. I was overwhelmed with joy at the gift of a camera one year! Grandmother and Granddaddy gave us gifts too, usually shoes or clothes.

After all that fun, we still got to spend the day with Grandmother and

Granddaddy. Grandmother cooked a huge dinner with plenty of desserts. We would spend the whole day playing with our cousins in Grandmother's front yard. Christmas day was so wonderful I tried to make it last as long as I could. Even in bed Christmas night I delayed sleep as long as possible, trying to hold onto the joy of the day.

Yes, Christmas was wonderful. I have other wonderful memories too. Daddy used to sing a little song to make us laugh. The words went like this, "Oh Joon, you look just like a goon, who sits upon the moon, Oh Joon, and I don't want to spoon, with a goon upon the moon, so I will leave you soon! Oh Joon." I would literally roll on the floor with the faces he made.

There were hot summer days when Daddy would buy us ten cent cups of ice cream from Dairy Queen. There were boxes of fresh donuts after early morning Sunday Mass. There was the father/daughter breakfast Daddy took me to in the second grade. There was the time in church when I almost fainted and Daddy got me out in the fresh air just in time. I remember the patient hours he spent driving Camp Fire Girls home from meetings and the surprise birthday party when I was twelve years old.

Maybe, like me, you have special memories too. Maybe you are tempted to believe that your abuse was not so bad after all. Maybe you are confused because there was love and family times and you cannot reconcile those times with the molestation. It is hard to accept the molestation when there are these bittersweet memories. The abuse memories don't make sense. They don't match the good times.

Some of my happiest childhood memories are of my parent's music. I spent many contented hours listening to them sing. I remember family sing-a-longs. All of us children harmonized with Mommy and Daddy and it was wonderful. During those times I felt so warm and loved, so protected.

The craziness flourishes in the best of times. Perfect childhood memories can be tainted with trauma lurking just below the surface. Don't allow the good memories to cover up the bad. Abuse is not removed because there were loving times. It can be even more difficult to get in touch with your feelings because of the loving times. Don't be tempted to doubt your painful memories because there are good memories. Cherish the good, but don't ignore the bad. There was still dysfunction, there was still pain. Allow yourself to accept the total truth about your past.

CHAPTER FORTY-THREE
WHICH WAY DO I GO?

So, what drove me into counseling? At what point did my life become unmanageable? I have pondered these questions and tried to come up with an answer, to perhaps even provide a map of my journey toward wholeness.

My life was always unmanageable. For a long time, I didn't understand that. There were always reasons for my dysfunction and my failures. My family didn't love me. My boss didn't understand me. I couldn't drive because I was uncoordinated. The list goes on and on. I didn't feel validated or understood by other people. I was never given the opportunities as a child that I should have had. I could make a hundred excuses for the problems in my life.

I finally understood my need to take control of my life when depression and regret hemmed me into a corner from which there was no escape. I was on the verge of changing jobs yet again. I couldn't deal with my employer's expectations and I felt childlike despair. I fell into a depression and once again started drinking and smoking. I felt that my relationships with my husband and my son were dying. In short, I came to a point where I no longer cared to live and function in this world. Pain drove me to do something about my circumstances and my crumbling internal world.

My first and most difficult step toward recovery involved picking up a phone and calling out for help. Since I was a Christian at that time with strong fundamentalist beliefs, I reached out to a pastor and started a course of pastoral counseling. That was not a good beginning for me. It was not the answer to my issues. Talking with my pastor glorified him and fed his ego. Just talking about the incidents that I remembered started a pattern of reliving memories that had long been buried in my past.

As I stated, counseling with my pastor was a bad beginning. There were many answers that he could not give me not having been trained as a therapist. He did not understand my deeply rooted rage, and the hatred that I sometimes manifested toward my parents conflicted with his belief that we must love and forgive. He urged me to forgive and forget. I could not, so I found myself in danger of coming into guilt and condemnation by the very person I had turned to for help.

I began listening to programming that dealt with incest and abuse on the radio. I was fortunate in hearing some wonderful counseling by counselors who understood that dealing with rage and hatred were an important part of the healing process. I would call and receive valuable advice from those caring counselors. Since I did not have the funds to go into clinical counseling, I began to search for answers on my own. I read as many books on inner healing as I could get my hands on. Through my self-education I began to understand the importance of writing out my memories and my dreams. I began to keep a journal and I wrote down my feelings, my dreams, and my memories.

As far as feelings are concerned, I discovered another area where I had rage toward my mother. Will I ever stop discovering these areas? When I had my first tubal pregnancy, I really, really, wanted her to be with me in the hospital. She had moved away from California and did not tell me. I kept begging Charles to call her. He really tried. He kept getting a disconnected message. I was so hurt. I wanted her. I needed her. I find that I have a hard time letting go of this pain. Another loss, I lost my baby and I lost my mother's caring. This was just another incident in a long line of incidents that add up to one conclusion. She did not love me the way I wanted her to love me. I need to accept this. It is so hard. I am still angry. This incident is an example of the work I continue to do to become whole. Part of the journey for me is to learn to accept my mother the way she was, not the way I wanted her to be. Forgiving my mother is essential to my recovery. I need to forgive her for me. Carrying all that anger depletes my energy. If I can become free from the anger and the hurt, I can move on to more productive issues in my life. I have made this discovery by using my journal as a tool. My journal also provides a record of my recovery. I can look back on my entries and see how far I've moved toward being well.

When I found a therapist, I could afford I was extremely lucky. She knew how to treat depression and DID. I had to learn how to talk about my abuse. After years of comparative silence on the subject of my traumas, I began to tell my current husband, Terry specific incidents from my childhood. I also introduced my alters to him. From him, I received essential support and understanding. Finding him so receptive gave me the courage to reach out to others.

Through my therapist and talking with other survivors I began to understand that I would always carry scars from my abuse. I would always suffer from panic attacks, but as time went by, I would learn how to manage them. The panic attacks would diminish in intensity and frequency. Through interacting with my therapist, I learned that I had not only one, but several inner children. These children within were often fearful and confused. By speaking out about them to my therapist I learned to sooth the fears of my inner children and to listen to them when they were in pain. I no longer suffer from DID. The children who were fearful are now part of my oneness. I am still releasing their pain. [1]

I found my therapist a safe and healthy way to continue counseling. I have been able to talk about and relive incidents of abuse in the safety her office. She and my husband provided the family and the unconditional love that I have always needed.

Recovery is a continuing process and I have been in recovery for about 17 years. I began a campaign of self-education, talking about my experiences, keeping a journal, and sharing with others. I found a therapist.

Still working I have nightmares and I am still recovering memories. I am still discovering who I am. I still have problems with authority figures. I accept that these issues are part of my life, but I can truly say that they are much less intense than they used to be. I have made progress and I will continue to make progress.

I am learning to deal with my feelings of guilt and shame. I can see real progress in my willingness to share with you, the reader, my life story. Writing my story has not been easy. Being honest about the incidents in my life has sometimes been hell. But writing my story has been very healing for me, I knew I had to write it in order to get on

---

[1] This statement is untrue. I later discovered that all my alters still exist. Rather than becoming one they have all agreed to speak in one voice. They are cooperative with one another.

with my own journey of recovery. Hopefully, sharing it will benefit you as well as me. Recovery is not some magical process that takes away all our pain. It takes hard work and commitment and a willingness to invest months, perhaps even years to learning how to live and manage our lives. Recovery is discovering who we should have been, had we not lived so many years in trauma. I can tell you that recovery is worth the pain of becoming whole. Recovery will help you to discover what your life should be.

CHAPTER FORTY-FOUR
WHAT CAN I DO TO BE WHOLE?

The sharing of my story is to provide hope. The key to remember is that recovery is a progressive process that continues throughout our lives. Through recovery we shape and mold ourselves us into the person we were meant to be. Every phase of the journey is worth the effort.

During the course of my journey I have learned many things about myself. I have learned that I am co-dependent, that I have had compulsive behaviors, and I have had poor boundaries. I am also an alcoholic and recovering from alcohol has become a large part of my recovery. I have made use of counseling, books on co-dependency, support groups, journalizing, seminars, and the safety of good friends to work out much of my recovery. I have poured my heart out in support groups and cried in the arms of trusted and loving friends. I have shared with my therapist my deep pain.

In your search for recovery, don't underestimate the significance of dreams. Write them in your journal and share them with your therapist. I had the following dream.

I was in the house in Texas, the house I grew up in. I saw myself as an adult, standing off to one side at the back of the living room. I saw the old orange couch. I saw my father's gray, metal desk. I saw the C.B. radio and the old piano. I also saw my grandfather sitting in a large, green easy chair. I was watching him closely because he held a small girl on his lap. She looked to be about four or five years old. She had short, straight hair and pretty brown eyes. She was wearing a shirt and a little pair of shorts. Her tiny feet were bare.

I did not know who this little girl was, but I was watching closely to make sure my grandfather did not molest her. It was never safe for me to sit on my grandfather's lap. I remember that he would squeeze me in areas that were private. I remember the feeling of his erection when he held me. As I watched him, the little girl knelt on his lap.

She wound her arms about his neck and kissed him on the cheek. He smiled and held her in a loving and protective manner. There was nothing even remotely sexual about his touch.

As I watched the two of them, my anger began to grow. I was angry because Granddaddy had never held me in such a safe and loving manner. I could not understand why he would protect this child when he had molested both me and my mother.

I woke from this dream feeling vaguely disturbed. Why was I dreaming about my grandfather and the house of molestation and rape, the house of fear and pain? Why was I dreaming of the house I grew up in? I searched these questions. Slowly, the answers began to come.

I was the little girl in the dream. I had never been protected and loved in such a way. As an adult I watched myself as the child being protected and held safely. My inner growth was showing that I was loved. All that I had missed would be restored to me. Oh, I would never be a child held safely in my grandfather's arms, but my inner parent would hold me safely in her arms. She would comfort the little ones who lived inside of my mind and body. She would give me back the joy of my stolen childhood. She would keep me safe.

Through meditation and therapy, I matured enough to protect the innocent children who lived inside of me. The parent Christine gently showed me how she was watchful and protective of the little ones. She loved them tenderly.; She only wanted good things for them. My therapist showed me that I must continue to heal from the anger the abuse has left inside of me. As I trusted myself and saw myself holding the child safe, I began to heal from that anger.

What does restoration mean? For each of us it is different. I believe that I will receive back what was stolen. I believe that I am getting back the things of my childhood. I am discovering the joy and wonder of being alive. I am locating the original, joyous child who was buried under all the rubble. She is blooming with confidence and security.

I am finding close and loving friends who hear the cries of my wounded heart   I am in a season of healing and renovation.

Ever so gently I am removing the dirt and rubble of my life, sifting through the mess to find treasures that might otherwise be lost I have slowly brought the damaged pieces to life and repaired them with infinite care. For me, it has been a process of seeing memories, feeling pain, and discovering the truth.

My recovery has been a process of restoration. The process is continuously ongoing. Sometimes it has been painful. Sometimes it has briefly halted for inclement weather. But it has been a process. It has been a journey. I have used the journey to learn many important things about myself.   I have strengthened the foundation and built slowly...

You may experience seasons of healing. You may struggle and cry out under an onslaught of memories that leave you gasping in pain and leave you crying. You may need to be in therapy. You may need to be in a safe hospital program for a season. Whatever direction you take in recovery you will discover the truth about you.

So, what can you do? What if there are no support groups in your area? How do you find a good counselor? What if you don't have money for professional counseling? Two or three good friends make a beautiful support group. Some of my deepest healing has been done in intimate groups of three or four. Begin by simple sharing of pain. You don't have to have all the answers. Just by listening to one another and supporting one another, sharing in the common areas of your pain, you can begin a beautiful healing inside of you. Healing begins by <u>sharing</u> our hurts. Sharing builds trust.

If you do a little investigating, you will probably find that there is quality counseling available at affordable rates. Some state programs use interns and supplement the cost of counseling with state funds. You may have to pay only a small portion. There are counselors available that operate on a sliding scale. Your payments are adjusted by your income. It is important that you seek out a counselor who understands your specific issues. Don't hesitate to ask if the counselor specializes in incest, sexual abuse, physical abuse, victimization, or whatever your specific need is.

Support groups provide a safe atmosphere to share. I would also like to mention that there are excellent hospital programs available for those who need a safe place to heal from deep wounds. If you have DID it is important that you find a therapist who can help you heal from the fragmentation. Your recovery journey will be special. Please, care about yourself and search for the counselor who can meet your intimate needs.

If you are experiencing periods of depression and a strong desire to commit suicide, I implore you to reach out for help immediately. You may need the safety of a hospital program for a while. Some insurance policies do cover this type of hospitalization. If you are struggling with these feelings, please a contact your local hotline or call 911. There is hope for you. You can get past the pain you are feeling now. But, please, reach out to somebody. Don't try to bear your despair alone.

Please realize you are not alone. There is hope and healing for you. Start your journey, it is worth the adventure. Reach out, call someone, and take care of yourself. Be filled with hope. In time you will shine!

Printed in Great Britain
by Amazon